THE ULTIMATE GUIDE TO

MAKING CHILI

THE ULTIMATE GUIDE TO
MAKING
CHILI

Easy and Delicious Recipes to Spice Up Your Diet

KATE ROWINSKI

PHOTOGRAPHS BY **JIM ROWINSKI**

Skyhorse Publishing

Skyhorse Publishing books may be purchased in bulk at special discounts for sales promotion, corporate gifts, fund-raising, or educational purposes. Special editions can also be created to specifications.
For details, contact the Special Sales Department, Skyhorse Publishing, 307 West 36th Street, 11th Floor, New York, NY 10018 or info@skyhorsepublishing.com.
Skyhorse and Skyhorse Publishing are registered trademarks of Skyhorse Publishing, Inc., a Delaware corporation.

www.skyhorsepublishing.com

10 9 8 7 6 5 4 3 2 1

Library of Congress Cataloging-in-Publication Data is available on file.

ISBN: 978-1-62087-189-8

Printed in China

Contents

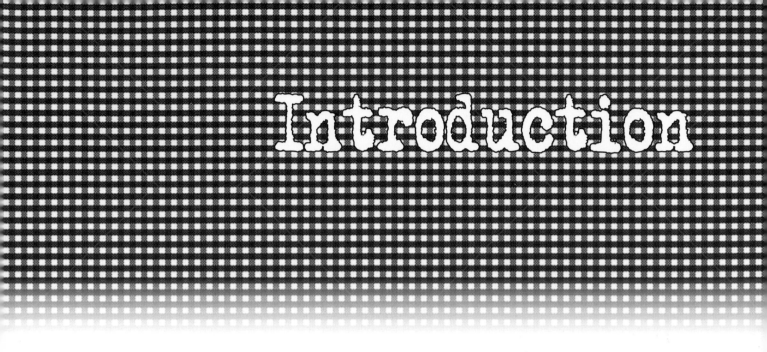

Introduction

Chili recipes inspire passion. Chili purists, often known as "chiliheads," declare that the only "real" chili is one made with meat and chile peppers—the fundamentals of the classic Texas "bowl of red." For many of us, the more traditional chili of tomatoes, ground meat, and beans forms our idea of the perfect bowl. Still others take great liberties, creating concoctions made entirely of vegetables, or creating fanciful lobster, squash, or bean stews. Championships are decided at cook-offs, competitions are won at potlucks and football game buffets, and loyalties are declared in the home kitchen.

But whether you like it hot or mild, white or red, beanless or vegetarian, there is one thing that every chili recipe depends upon—and that is the chile pepper.

Introduction to the Chile Pepper

IT'S ALL IN THE HEAT

Chiles come in a wide and sometimes bewildering variety of colors, shapes, and sizes. To complicate matters further, chiles are sometimes eaten green, sometimes ripened. They can be eaten fresh, dried, canned, or ground and blended. With so many options, from the mild bell pepper to the off-the-charts ghost chile, there is a taste and style for nearly every palate.

Virtually all peppers share one fundamental ingredient: capsaicin. It is capsaicin that gives the chili its distinctive heat. Capsaicin is held in the fleshy meat of the pepper, with higher concentrations at the top of the stem, through the veins, and around the seeds. (The one exception is the bell pepper, whose mild taste forms the bottom of the heat index.)

Until 1912, there was pretty much only one way to determine how hot a chile pepper was—and that was to bite into it. That experience could be in turns painful or disappointing depending on what qualities one was seeking. Wilbur Scoville, a chemist at the Parke-Davis Pharmaceutical Company, changed all that with his Scoville scale, a measure of the amount of capsaicin in a chile. Today his scale is the standard by which all peppers are measured. While the true heat of a chile is affected by many factors, such as heat, humidity, soil conditions, and hybridization, the Scoville scale describes the average heat of a chile in relationship to others, allowing you a starting point in determining the type of pepper you would like to use. Chiles are rated in Scoville Heat Units, a number that describes the parts per million of capsaicin.

SAMPLING OF COMMON CHILE PEPPERS ON THE SCOVILLE SCALE

VARIETY	HEAT UNITS
Bell Pepper	0
Banana Pepper, Cubanelle	100–900
New Mexico, Anaheim	500–1,000
Ancho, Pasilla, Cascabel	1,000–2,500
Guajillo	2,500–5,000
Jalapeño, Chipotle	5,000–8,000
Serrano, Arbol	10,000–23,000
Cayenne, Tabasco	30,000–50,000
Thai Pepper	50,000–100,000
Habanero, Scotch Bonnet	100,000–350,000
Red Savina	350,000–580,000
Ghost Chile, Bhut Jolokia	855,000–1,359,000

SELECTING CHILES

So many chiles, so little time! With so many different chiles to choose from, how do you know where to start?

This is where the fun really begins. Do you want fresh, smoky, rich or just plain hot? A pasilla base will give you rich undertones; combined with an arbol kicker, you have glow-in-the-dark heat. An ancho base may suit the whole family, but add a split fresh jalapeño to the pot for the more adventurous diners.

Choose fresh chiles that are bright, smooth, and crisp. Shriveled skins, soft spots, and bruises indicate chiles that are past their prime.

When choosing dried whole chiles, look for good color and shiny skins. Dried chiles are good for about six months. All dried chiles are wrinkled, but watch out for those that look withered or old with faded color. (Dried chiles tend to be dusty. Clean whole chiles before using by wiping them with a damp cloth or rinsing them under running water.)

Some common chili-type chiles include:

New Mexico: Large chiles that can be used green or red, with a sweet, pungent, earthy flavor. Also sometimes called Anaheim; this mild chile that forms the basis of many traditional chili recipes.

Ancho: A dried poblano. The ancho is the sweetest of the dried chiles, making it perfect for red chili. Mildly spicy with a dark coffee-like bite.

Pasilla: A dried chilaca pepper that is spicy with a bitter undertone.

Cascabel: Small, deep-red chile known for its loose seeds that rattle when shaken. Nutty and medium hot with a slightly smoky flavor.

Guajillo: Smokier and spicier than the ancho, but with a fruity tanginess that surprises.

Chipotle: A red ripe jalapeño smoked over mesquite. The popular chipotle provides a smoky earthiness with underlying heat.

De Arbol: Very hot red dried chile that can substitute easily for cayenne.

Habanero: Fiery hot and not for the faint of heart. A little goes a long way.

Ghost chile: Not so common, but worth noting. The ghost chile is arguably the hottest chile in the world. It is unlikely you will be cooking with it, but it makes a nice piece of chile trivia. Of course, eating one gives you definite bragging rights among your heat-loving friends.

GROWING CHILES

Though they are native to the tropics, chile peppers can be grown in most areas of the United States. A little more tolerant of cold weather than tomatoes and eggplants, they do want some hot weather to produce at their best.

The best conditions for really hot chile varieties are hot conditions, climates where 90 degree summer days are common. Chiles don't have a lot of natural enemies, so they are generally pretty easy to grow.

Light watering is all that is really needed, along with a little liquid seaweed. Too much nitrogen-rich fertilizer may result in spectacular leaves but lower fruit production. Seedlings can be started indoors or purchased at the local nursery and then transplanted when warmer conditions set in. A single chile plant can also do well in a container.

We plant a lot of chile peppers, both mild and hot varieties, and keep them pretty close together. They do cross-pollinate, and we have found some interesting varieties of heat the following year in the Anaheim seeds that were planted near the jalapeños. You can pick your chiles throughout the season, starting when they are still green. (Picking them when they are small actually stimulates fruit production in the plant.) If your growing season is long enough, allow as many as possible to ripen fully to achieve their full heat.

To save seeds for next year, remove the seeds from raw, ripened peppers. Rinse seeds and set them out in the sun to dry. When they are completely dry, package and label in envelopes.

HANDLING CHILES

Handle chiles carefully! Hot chiles contain oils that can really burn if they come in contact with your mouth, nose, or eyes. Here are a few tips for keeping yourself comfortable in the chile kitchen:

Always wear rubber gloves when cutting or peeling chiles. If you use the disposable type, peel off and discard inside out, and immediately wash your hands. If you use the heavier reusable gloves, wash them thoroughly with soap and water before removing them from your hands.

Use only cutting boards and bowls made from non-porous materials. If you do use a plastic or wood cutting board, keep one that is dedicated only to chiles.

Turn away from the food processor or stove top when chopping or sautéing chiles to avoid a lungful of stinging vapors. Likewise, never cut chiles under running water.

Consider charring or toasting your chiles on an outside grill to keep vapors out of the house entirely. This is not too important for a couple of chiles, but if you are doing a large batch, everyone will thank you.

Red chile stains rubber and nylon spatulas and bowls. Soak them overnight in a weak solution of bleach and water.

To remove the oils from your hands, scrub them together with cold water and a teaspoon of salt. Then wash them using regular soap and water.

There's not much help for the burn of a chile, but experts agree that milk-based products do the best job in counteracting a mouthful of the spicy stuff.

ROASTING AND PEELING GREEN CHILES

To bring out their flavor, mild green chiles should be roasted and peeled before using. (It is not necessary to use this method for hot green chiles like jalapeños or serranos.)

Roasting and peeling chiles is a fairly labor-intensive activity. If you have a gas stove, you can do a few chiles directly over the gas burner. But a batch of chiles is most easily done over a barbecue grill.

To prepare chiles for roasting, wash chiles and make a small slit in each one to allow steam to escape.

Using a set of tongs, place chiles over open flame or on a hot grill for 5–6 minutes, turning to blister all sides. A little blackening may occur, but you are not looking for a burnt appearance, just enough blistering to allow them to be easily peeled. As each chile is finished, remove it from grill and place in a roasting pan covered with a damp towel. This steams the chiles slightly and will help with peeling. When chiles are cool, peel them under running water as you would a hard-boiled egg, flaking off the charred skin from the stem downward. Then remove stem, slit, and remove seeds.

FREEZING CHILES

Inevitably there comes a point when there are just entirely too many chiles in the garden! We dry all the thinner-skinned varieties, like the Pueblos and the cayenne. Thicker-skinned varieties can also be dried, but I eventually resort to freezing some of the thicker-skinned peppers. Some people prepare peppers for freezing by seeding them and cutting them into strips. I just wash and dry them whole and put them in a zip freezer bag. They are a bit mushy when they are thawed, but they retain great flavor and the skin slides right off.

DRYING CHILES

If you are in a climate conducive to their needs, chiles require nothing more than fresh air and sunshine to dry beautifully. The southwestern United States, where the hot sun and low humidity make conditions ideal for drying chiles, produces beautiful strands of decorative ristras—strands of glorious dried red chiles. Ristras are generally used for decorative purposes, although a fresh strand of ristras can be hung in the kitchen for use for about 6 months.

Start with fresh, healthy, ripened chiles. Remove any chiles that are past their prime or show signs of bruising or other damage.

To air-dry chiles:

If your climate provides hot, sunny conditions and relatively low humidity for most of the day, consider air-drying your chiles.

Slice chiles in half lengthwise, stem, and remove seeds. Use a window screen as your drying board. Place chiles cut side down and lay out in the sun as early in the day as you can so you can take advantage of the most sun. A porch roof or a truck bed is an ideal place to dry chiles. Allow chiles to dry on one side all day. At night, cover the screens with a light sheet, or bring inside if you think the evening will be cool or damp. The next day, turn the chiles over and repeat the process.

Drying time varies due to weather conditions and size of chile. A properly dried chile should be completely free of moisture, with a leathery, almost brittle texture.

To oven-dry chiles:

In cooler or more humid conditions, oven-drying provides a more reliable method for producing consistently good chiles.

Turn oven on to the lowest heat, about 200 degrees. Slice chiles in half lengthwise, stem, and remove seeds. Place on cookie sheets and leave in oven all day or overnight. Check them occasionally, turning over as needed. Larger chiles can take as long as 48 hours to reach the perfect dryness, but most will be done within 24 hours.

GRINDING CHILES

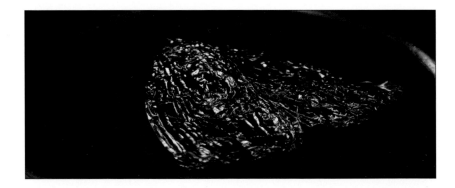

Prepare your whole dried chiles for grinding by cleaning them, either by hand-dusting or with a quick rinse under running water. Place a dry cast iron griddle over high heat and toast chiles on both sides to stiffen the outside of the chile so that it will crack easily. Remove from heat and cool slightly, then break off stem, slit each chile lengthwise, and remove seeds. Tear into pieces and grind to a fine powder. Traditionalists use a mortar and pestle. I keep a coffee grinder dedicated for the purpose.

Grind chiles by type, or choose a combination of chiles to create your own signature blend. Ground chile is best if used immediately, but you can store leftovers in glass containers out of direct light.

RECONSTITUTING CHILES

Choose the chile pods you would like in your paste. You can use all one type, but it is fun to make combinations to suit your taste. I like to take the relatively mild, sweet ancho and add some hotter, smokier guajillo. A ratio of 2 anchos to 1 guajillo would be a good starting point. Remember you can always make something hotter, but it is much harder to cool it down.

Remove stems and split the chiles to remove the seeds. A sharp knife or kitchen shears works well for this. If you want to cool down especially hot chiles, remove as much of the veins inside as you can; that's where much of the capsaicin lives. Do this by opening up the chile, laying it flat and scraping the interior lightly.

Heat a dry cast iron skillet and place each chile flat on the surface, turning once to heat both sides, just to bring out the aroma of the chile. It will deepen in color, but make sure not to char them; burned chiles will make a bitter paste. This process should take less than 45 seconds on each side.

Place the chiles in a bowl and add hot water, just enough to cover. Soak for about 30 minutes. Drain chiles and discard the bitter juice. Puree the softened chiles in a food processor to make a paste.

You can use your chile paste in place of dried chili powder at this point. One whole dried ancho or chile of equivalent size equals about one tablespoon ground chile.

COMMERCIAL CHILI POWDERS

With so many different chiles to choose from, how do you know where to start? The first thing to do is understand the language of the ground dried chile. Not everyone adheres strictly to these terms, but they give you an idea what to look for.

The term **ground chile** is generally used to describe pure dried chiles. These are sold by specific chile variety, such as ancho ground chili powder. Many people find that they can get all the variety they need by keeping one mild chili powder and one hot chili powder in their pantry.

Ground chile blends are a combination of mild and hot chiles created to provide certain flavors and levels of heat, and allow you to achieve consistent results.

Chili powder (note the *i* instead of the *e* at the end) refers to a combination of ground chile, cumin, garlic or any variety of other seasonings. Much of what you find in the grocery store is this sort of blend, an uncertain combination of preservatives and too much salt. But there are wonderful chili blends on the market.

If you are just starting out, there is no better place to begin than at Pendery's. They carry a wide array of chile products, including ground chile, chile blends, and chili powder. Try Pendery's Chile Assortment Packs to give yourself exposure to several different blends. Pendery's has been making chile blends since the 1800s and provide some of the best on the market. Find them at www. penderys.com.

Chili-Making Basics

SELECT YOUR EQUIPMENT

The chili pot. A wide, heavy-bottomed pot is essential for making good chili. A thick bottom conducts heat gently and evenly throughout the searing and simmering process. Choose one with straight sides and plenty of surface area for searing your meat. We use copper in our kitchen, but there are plenty of aluminum and clad choices that will fit the bill. Cast iron is not a good choice for chili for a couple of reasons. First, the iron in the pot can influence the chili's flavor. Second, the interior surface of seasoned cast iron does not tend to react well to the tomato in some chili recipes. Though I do use cast iron outdoors from time to time, I am quick to clean and re-oil the surface afterwards. Your pot will probably come with a lid, but for most recipes, we simmer our chili uncovered. A similarly heavyweight skillet will also come in handy for toasting whole chile peppers.

A good knife. Classic chilies feature small chunks of meat, generally in ½" to 1" cubes. Cubing several pounds of meat can be rather time consuming, particularly if you are concerned

with consistency in the size and shape of your cubes. A good quality chef's knife is essential. A chef's knife is designed with a sharp, wide blade that is gently sloped to allow the blade to rock back and forth for dicing onions or mincing garlic. There are a number of factors to consider when choosing the best knife for your needs. Go to a good kitchen store for advice on knife construction and blade types, but don't settle for the highest price or the fanciest name brand. Once you have narrowed down your choices, choose the knife that feels most comfortable in your hand. It should be well balanced and not too heavy. I use a German-style 10 carbon steel chef's knife for most of my knife work.

A meat grinder. We make all our own ground meat at the restaurant and we carry that habit to our home kitchen. There are a few reasons for this. First, when we grind our own meat, we know exactly what's in it. We understand the amount of fattiness it contains, as well as the quality of the cuts used, and we are sure of its freshness. Second, grinding it ourselves allows us to do the grind that best suits our needs. Though any ground meat will work in chili, a coarse grind is the most traditional. Some butchers will do a coarse grind for you, but we like the control we get with our own grinder. Lastly, we like to grind our own meat for the blends we can make. I sometimes grind beef, pork, and veal together, and even occasionally add onions or garlic right in with the meat. There are electric and manual grinders on the market. I grew up with the manual style, but have converted to the food grinder attachment on my KitchenAid.

A burr grinder. For the freshest-tasting chili powder and to create our own signature blends, we often grind our own dried chile peppers. We have a favorite mortar and pestle made of wood that is reserved exclusively for grinding chile, but we also keep a dedicated electric grinder handy for the purpose. If you go the electric route, choose a good quality burr grinder—and don't be tempted to share it with your coffee beans! Neither your chili nor your morning cup of Joe will thank you for it!

CHOOSE YOUR MEAT

If we are talking about regulation Texas chili, then beef is the meat of choice. Traditional Texas chilies can be made with chunks of beef, coarsely ground beef, or a combination of the two. Chuck roast seems to be the perfect combination of flavor and fat, but the leaner cut of round will also work, as will brisket and sirloin. For pork chili, choose a nice pork shoulder.

Freeze your meat slightly to make it easier to cube or grind. To start, trim the meat of most of its fat and connective tissue, and set the scraps aside for making stock. The size of meat chunks is a matter of personal preference. I rather like the larger chunks, up to 1" in size, partly because I can get them cut more quickly, but also because I like the substance of a large piece in my bowl. My husband prefers ½" chunks, and as long as he is willing to stand and cut them, I am okay with that.

Most of my chili recipes call for about 3 pounds of meat. Our favorite family chili calls for both grind and chunks, and I am a fan of adding some pork into the grind to sweeten the flavor.

Of course, that is just the beginning when it comes to chili recipes. Wild game, chicken, turkey, and varieties of fish and seafood are all fair game for the chili pot. The main thing to remember is that while some fat is essential for flavor, too much fat can spoil the pot. So keep your choices on the lean side.

COMMERCIAL STOCK OR HOMEMADE?

You can certainly make a good chili with commercial stock, and even reconstituted bouillon cubes make an acceptable base liquid. We always make our own stock at the restaurant. We find that it adds a richness of flavor and texture that we can't get any other way.

BEEF STOCK

Olive oil
4 pounds meaty bones from the butcher
½ pound stew meat or trimming scraps
2 onions, peeled and quartered
2 carrots, peeled and cut into chunks
Celery tops or a couple of ribs
2–3 cloves garlic
Fresh parsley
2 bay leaves
8–10 peppercorns

Place bones, scraps, carrots, and onions in a large roasting pan and sprinkle all over with oil. Roast in 400 degree oven for about 45 minutes, turning occasionally until bones are nicely browned. Remove meat and vegetables from pan and place them in a large stock pot. De-glaze the roasting pan on top of the stove with ½ cup of water. Use a spatula to scrape the browned bits from the bottom of the pan. Add this to the stock pot. Add celery, garlic, parsley, bay leaves, and peppercorns. Fill the pot with water (to within 2" of the top) and cover loosely with foil. Bring to a boil, and then simmer on low heat for 3–4 hours.

Spoon excess fat from the top of the pot, remove the bones and vegetables, and strain stock into another pot through a fine mesh sieve. Let cool to room temperature and then refrigerate.

When ready to use, remove any solid fat from the top of the stock and discard. Freeze extra stock for later use.

CHICKEN STOCK

Leftover bones and skin from a roasted chicken
2 onions, peeled and quartered
2 carrots, peeled and cut into chunks
Celery tops or a couple of ribs
Fresh parsley
2 bay leaves
8–10 peppercorns

Place the chicken carcass and all the rest of the ingredients into a large stock pot and cover with cold water. Bring to a boil, and then simmer on low heat for 3–4 hours. Spoon excess fat from the top of the pot, remove the bones and vegetables, and strain stock into another pot through a fine mesh sieve. Let cool to room temperature and then refrigerate. When ready to use, remove any solid fat from the top of the stock and discard. Freeze extra stock for later use.

VEGETABLE STOCK

1 large onion, quartered
2–3 carrots, cut into chunks
Celery tops or a couple of ribs
3 cloves garlic
1 leek, green and white, chopped
1 parsnip
1 tomato, chopped
4–5 sprigs fresh thyme
1 bay leaf
1 bunch parsley
10 peppercorns

Place all the ingredients into a large stock pot and cover with cold water. Bring to a boil, and then simmer on low heat for 1–2 hours. Remove the vegetables, and strain stock into another pot through a fine mesh sieve. Let cool to room temperature and then refrigerate. Freeze extra stock for later use.

GATHER YOUR SPICES

The king of the chili pot is most definitely the chile pepper. So the first thing to decide is, how you are going to deliver that chile flavor to your pot? How hot do you want it? Do you have fresh chiles available or are you going to use dried chiles? Will you reconstitute dried chiles or grind them fresh? Do you want to blend different chiles together or do you just want to rely on a really good commercial chile blend? Any of these choices can be the basis for great chili—the choices are yours.

Consider making up a puree of your favorite chile pepper to spoon in toward the end of cooking or at the table. Add slowly until your desired heat is achieved. That last-minute splash of fresh heat makes an invigorating bowl.

In addition to your chiles, a handful of other spices will be a standard part of your chili pantry.

Garlic and onions are staple ingredients in most chilies. Some recipes call for off-the-shelf onion flakes and garlic powder. While I rely on them on we are camping, I personally prefer to use fresh onions and garlic. Before I start cooking, I place a large onion and about 3–5 garlic cloves in the food processor and puree them down to a fine blend, then set aside until ready to use.

Cumin can be used as whole seeds or in the ground form. Regular ground cumin is fine, but I like the fragrance and depth of roasted cumin for some recipes. You can roast the whole seeds lightly and grind them, or buy commercial roasted ground cumin.

Mexican oregano is a little different than its Mediterranean cousin. Mediterranean oregano has a savory pungency that immediately calls to mind Italian pasta sauces, while the Mexican version carries notes of lemon and even licorice. While your chili recipe can tolerate either one, find the Mexican if you can.

Ground cinnamon is the essential ingredient in Cincinnati chili, but you will find that it adds sparkle to many of your chili recipes. If you experiment with cinnamon, start with 1 teaspoon per 2 pounds of meat.

Fresh cilantro is a basic ingredient in many salsas and chilies. If you are cooking for a crowd though, be aware that people often have a strong reaction to this lovely herb. Those who love it experience it as fresh and citrusy, those who don't describe it as dirty dishwater. We love it in my household, so I often finely chop a whole bunch of cilantro with a little oil to make a paste. I add some to the pot and save some to garnish our bowls.

TO BEAN OR NOT TO BEAN?

Some people consider beans an essential part of the chili recipe, others would never add them, and still others consider a pot of chili beans a complete meal. Canned beans work fine in most recipes. Just make sure to drain the can and rinse the beans thoroughly to remove the excess starch. You will find a recipe for chili beans on page 64. Several bean varieties turn up in chili recipes. For the most part, beans like black, kidney, or pintos are pretty interchangeable, based entirely on your preference. White chili, of course, calls for lighter beans. Use Great Northern, navy, or cannellini beans.

BASIC BEANS

Cooking beans this way reduces the gassiness that some people associate with eating beans and also gives you nice, whole beans that are not broken or mushy.

1 cup dried beans, rinsed and cleaned (pinto, black, kidney, Great Northern, navy, or cannellini)
Water
Salt

Wash beans and make sure there are no small stones or other debris present. Place in a large bowl and cover with boiling water. Soak overnight.

The next morning, drain beans and rinse. Place back in pot, cover with fresh water, and bring to a boil. Once beans are boiling, continue to cook for about 5 minutes. Remove from heat, skim foam, drain, and rinse.

Place beans in fresh water, bring to a boil, then turn heat to low, and simmer for about 1 hour. (Kidney beans usually require a little more time so add about 15 minutes when cooking these. Navy may be ready in 45–50 minutes.) For quicker beans, cook in pressure cooker for about 8 minutes. Or if you have all day, place on low in crock pot for 6–8 hours.

When beans have reached desired doneness, drain them and season. Add salt only *after* cooking; beans cooked with salt tend to be a little tough. One cup of dried beans will yield 2½ cups or so. If you don't need your whole batch of beans at one time, place rinsed beans in zipper freezer bags and store leftovers in freezer for next time.

COOKING YOUR CHILI

Chili is actually a simple dish with only a few rules.

Sear your protein lightly. It doesn't need to be browned. Just make sure it is seared to an even gray before adding other ingredients.

See that nice juice forming at the bottom of the pot? Yummy! Leave it there. Hopefully you started with meat that was not too fatty, but any fat should stay in the pot during cooking. Fat binds the flavors together—some cooks even add a little suet or a tablespoon of oil to their chili during the cooking process. If you refrigerate your chili until the next day, a hard skim of fat may form on top. Just remove that before reheating.

Simmer and taste. What is the use of a beautifully fragrant chili sitting on top of the stove if you can't walk over and check it now and then? I usually start my recipe with about half of my spices and reserve the rest to adjust the pot as I taste it. Finish adding seasonings at least a half hour before you are done cooking. The spices need time to open up and incorporate themselves into the flavors.

The salt content of your chili will depend somewhat on the types of tomatoes, stock, or beans that you are using, so always taste before adding salt.

Is your pot too spicy? A bit of sugar or honey may help ease the burn. Add a teaspoon at a time to try taming the heat without over-sweetening the pot. (A bit of dark chocolate may also help.) At the table, serve with rice or refried beans to keep the burn down.

Beer and chili seem like logical companions, but it is dairy products that will help dull an overly spicy burn. Add a dollop of sour cream to a bowl of three-alarm chili or keep a glass of milk at hand.

If you are adding beans, add them during the last half hour.

Chili making is more art than science! Find a recipe you like, then play with your ingredients until you have it just the way you want it.

Make enough for leftovers. Chili is even better the next day!

Competitive Chili

I am by no means a competitive chili participant, although I have been to my share of competitions and love the spirit of camaraderie and competition that these events evoke. More of a festival of chili—you get to taste everyone's entries and often are allowed to vote for a "people's choice" that is awarded in addition to the judges' favorite.

Affectionately known as Chiliheads, competitive chili chefs cook, taste, and compete while helping to raise money and awareness for a wide range of charitable causes.

CHILI CLUBS

The International Chili Society and The Chili Appreciation Society International are non-profit organizations that sanction chili cook-offs worldwide, benefitting charities and non-profit organizations.

The ICS sanctions over 200 cook-offs with over one million people tasting, cooking, and judging. There are three sanctioned cook-off categories: Red (traditional red chili), Chili Verde (green chili), and Salsa. All winners of ICS-sanctioned cook-offs qualify to compete for cash prizes and awards at the World's Championship Chili Cookoff, held each year in October. The ICS annually crowns a World Champion in each category.

CASI sanctions over 500 chili cookoffs internationally each year as qualifying events for the Terlingua International Chili Championship, which is held in November in Terlingua, Texas.

CHILI CONTEST RULES

Contests over pots of chili can happen anywhere, from the company's potluck to the Super Bowl buffet. But if you want to compete in an official chili cook-off, here are some of the rules you can expect. (Go to the group's sponsoring site to get the official rules for a specific cook-off.)

Traditional red chili is generally defined as any kind of meat or combination of meats, cooked with red chili peppers, various spices, and other ingredients. Chili Verde is defined as any kind of meat or combination of meats, cooked with green chili peppers, various spices, and other ingredients. Unless there is a home-style category, beans, pasta, and other fillers are forbidden.

No ingredient may be pre-cooked in any way prior to the commencement of the official cook-off, with the exception of canned or bottled tomatoes, tomato sauce, peppers, pepper sauce, beverages, broth, and grinding and/or mixing of spices. If salsa is in the recipe, it must be homemade by the contestant.

The regulation cooking period will usually be 3–4 hours. You will be expected to provide a minimum amount of chili for judging. Judges will base their decision on flavor, texture of the meat, consistency, blend of spices, aroma, and color. Depending on the contest, you will probably also need to provide a separate pot of chili for visitor tastings.

COMPETITION CHILI RECIPES

This is the way the big boys (and girls) do it. Below are some of the World Championship recipes for the past several years, compliments of the International Chili Society.

There is something magical that happens when you make a good pot of chili; a kind of alchemy of atmosphere, equipment, ingredients, and cook's charm that makes every pot unique.

There's a saying on the competitive circuit, "You can make someone's recipe, but you can't make their chili." Try one of these recipes yourself, and compare the champions' styles. Then try to come up with your own magical brew. Want to try a competition yourself? Go to www.chilicookoff.com or www.chili.org to find competitions in your area.

JOHN'S CHILI

2011 World's Championship Chili Cookoff Winner—John Jepson

3 pounds (1.36 kg) lean tri-tip, ¼ inch cubes
1-10 ounce (300 ml) can Swanson's Chicken Broth
1 cup (240 ml) Swanson's Beef Broth
2 tablespoons (12 g) Rancho De Chimayo Hot New Mexico Chili powder
2 chicken bouillon cubes
½ cup (120 ml) Hunt's Tomato Sauce
3 tablespoons (22 g) medium hot New Mexico chili powder
4 tablespoons (30 g) quality chili powder
1 tablespoon (7.5 g) garlic powder
1 ½ tablespoons (11 g) onion powder
1 teaspoon (5 g) Sea Salt
¼ cup (60 ml) Hunt's Tomato Sauce
3 tablespoons (22 g) mild California chili powder
½ tablespoon (3 g) hot New Mexico chili powder
1 tablespoon (6 g) cumin
2 tablespoons (18 g) cornstarch
1 teaspoon (5 g) Sea Salt

Rinse the blood off of the meat. Lightly brown tri-tip in small batches until gray in color and add to pot. Add next 5 ingredients, bring to a boil, cover and reduce to a light boil for 2 hours or until meat is very tender. Add the next 6 ingredients and turn to a very low simmer for 30 minutes. Add the next 5 ingredients and leave at a very low simmer for 30 minutes.

You may adjust to taste by adding small amounts of cayenne or red tabasco, cumin, salt or brown sugar. Add chicken broth as necessary to cover meat. Simmer until tender.

*For a smoother sauce, run powders through a spice grinder and soak them in a very small amount of chicken broth.

HAPPY TRAILS! CHILI

2010 World's Championship Chili Cookoff Winner—Thomas H. Hoover, Jr.

2¾ pounds (1.25 kg) tri-tip sirloin beef cut in 3/8″ cubes
1-15 ounce (443 ml) can beef broth
1-8 ounce (237 ml) can chicken broth
1-8 ounce (237 ml) can tomato sauce
1 tablespoon (7.5 g) granulated onion
1 tablespoon (7.5 g) granulated garlic
1 tablespoon (7.5 g) pasilla chili powder
4 tablespoons (30 g) Gebhardt chili powder
3 tablespoons (22 g) California chili powder
1 tablespoon (7.5 g) New Mexico chili powder
1 tablespoon (6 g) cumin
1 fresh minced serrano chili pepper
2 teaspoons (10 g) salt

Brown meat, drain fat and juice, add to pot. Add both broths and tomato sauce and simmer ½ hour. Add other ingredients and simmer covered until meat is tender. Add 2 tablespoons (15 g) Happy Trails Chili Seasoning Mix and simmer 5 minutes. Check for salt.

MAUREEN'S ALMOST FAMOUS RED CHILI

2009 World's Championship Chili Cookoff Winner—Maureen Barrett

3 pounds (1.36 kg) of tri-tip cubed
1-8 ounce (237 ml) can tomato sauce
1-15 ounce (443 ml) can of chicken broth
⅛ teaspoon (.5 g) red pepper powder
1 teaspoon (3 g) chicken base
2 tablespoons (15 g) Gebhardt's chili powder
2 tablespoons (15 g) Ray's brand chili powder
1-15 ounce (443 ml) can beef broth
1 tablespoon (7.5 g) Ray's brand onion powder
1 whole jalapeño seeded and halved
½ teaspoon (2.5 g) white pepper
1 packet Sazon goya seasoning
½ teaspoon (2.5 g) salt
3 tablespoons (22 g) Gebhart's chili powder
1 tablespoon (7.5 g) Ray's brand garlic powder
2 tablespoons (12 g) Ray's brand cumin
¼ teaspoon (1.25 g) brown sugar
1 tablespoon (7.5 g) New Mexico light chili powder
1 teaspoon (3 g) Ray's brand cumin
2 tablespoons (15 g) New Mexico light chili powder
1 tablespoon (7.5 g) Gebhardt's chili powder
Thicken with arrowroot
salt or brown sugar to taste
tomato sauce if needed

Brown cut up tri-tip in pot until gray in color. Add the next 9 ingredients, bring it to a boil, cover and simmer for one hour. Add the next 7 ingredients and cook for another 30 minutes before adding the brown sugar, New Mexico light chili powder and cumin. Continue to simmer pot for another 30 minutes.

20 minutes before turn in, add the remaining ingredients adjusting taste with the salt or brown sugar and tomato sauce if needed.

SOUTHERN CHILI

2008 World's Championship Chili Cookoff Winner—Georgia Weller

4 tablespoons (30 g) California chili powder
3 tablespoons (22 g) Gebhardt's chili powder
1 tablespoon (7.5 g) pasilla chili powder
1 tablespoon (7.5 g) Chimayo chili powder
2½ tablespoons (15 g) cumin
1 tablespoon (7.5 g) granulated garlic
1 tablespoon (7.5 g) onion powder
½ teaspoon (2 g) cayenne powder
2 teaspoons (10 g) salt

Combine above ingredients for spice mix. Reserve 4 tablespoons of mix and set aside. Divide the remaining amount into 2 equal parts.

3 pounds (1.36 kg) Tri-Tip roast or Chuck Tender cut in small chunks
1-15 ounce (443 ml) can of beef broth (Swanson's)
1-15 ounce (443 ml) can of chicken broth (Swanson's)
1-10 ounce (300 ml) can of tomato puree (Hunt's)
2 whole green chiles from a can of whole ones, blended
Tabasco to taste
Salt to taste

In chili pot, combine beef broth, chicken broth, tomato puree and ½ of remaining spice mix.
In skillet, brown the meat, drain, and add to chili pot. Cook for about 1½ hours. Add other ½ of spice mix and blended green chiles and simmer for an additional hour. Add reserved 4 tablespoons (25 g) of spice mix and cook a half hour more or until meat is tender. Adjust salt if necessary. Add Tabasco to taste.

BOOMAS REVENGE

2007 World's Championship Chili Cookoff Winner—Jerry Buma

3 pounds (1.36 kg) tri-tip steak
1 medium onion, minced
1-4 ounce (115 g) can green chiles, diced
3 cloves garlic, minced
1-10 ounce (300 ml) can chicken broth
1½ teaspoons (7.5 ml) Tabasco
1-8 ounce (237 ml) can Hunt's tomato sauce

Blend together:
2 tablespoons (15 g) Mexico hot powder
2 tablespoons (15 g) Mexico mild powder
2 tablespoons (15 g) California hot powder
2 tablespoon (15 g) California mild powder
3 tablespoons (18 g) cumin
1 teaspoon (5 g) black pepper
2 teaspoon (10 g) salt
1 teaspoon (5 g) sugar
2 teaspoons (8 g) MSG
1 teaspoon (3 g) Mexican oregano

Brown meat in small batches; return to pot with veggies, chicken broth, and half the spice mix. Simmer 2 hrs. Add remaining spice mix and cook for 1 hr. adding liquid if necessary. Adjust seasonings to personal taste last 15 min.

J.R.'S ROUGH AND READY CHILI

2006 World's Championship Chili Cookoff Winner—J.R. Knudson

3 pounds (1.36 kg) beef tri-tip, chopped
2 ounces (56 g) sausage
1 ounce (28 g) rendered beef fat
1 medium onion, diced
1 tablespoon (7.5 g) garlic powder
1 green Ortega pepper, remove seeds and dice fine
½ teaspoon (2.5 g) salt
¼ teaspoon (1 g) fine black pepper
2 ounces (15 g) Gebhardt chili powder
½ ounce (3.5 g) California chili powder
½ ounce (3.5 g) New Mexico powder
½ ounce (3 g) cumin
½ teaspoon (2 g) pequin powder
2-14 ounce (415 ml) cans chicken broth
1-6 ounce (177 ml) can Hunt's Tomato Sauce
¼ teaspoon (1 g) cayenne pepper
Tabasco sauce to taste

Sauté onion and green pepper in rendered beef fat in a 3-quart (2.8 L) pot. Add garlic powder and half of chili powder. Add half a can of chicken broth, mix well and set aside. Brown sausage and beef in a skillet about one pound at a time. Drain and add meat to onion mix. Add remaining chili powder and remaining can of chicken broth. Cook for 30 minutes on low heat. Add tomato sauce, cumin, cayenne pepper, and pequin powder. Add more broth as needed and cook until meat is tender, about two to three hours. Add a dash of Tabasco sauce if needed for heat.

Traditional Chili

When it comes to chili, the use of the word "traditional" may be enough to start a heated debate. But it seems pretty certain that people have been combining meat, tomatoes and chile peppers for centuries–probably originally in Spanish cooking. How the cowboys latched onto it is not entirely clear, although the ready availability of chile peppers in the American southwest and the easy portability of dried chiles suspended in bricks of suet probably were an appealing alternative to the bland campfire diet.

Over the years, that original blend of meat and chile peppers has spread across the United States, being tweaked and modified as available ingredients and individual palates saw fit. Beans were almost certainly introduced as an inexpensive alternative to meat, and tomatoes were added to sweeten and soften the flavor. As immigrants tasted and modified it, cinnamon and other seasonings were added.

This chapter features the basics—the place all chili variations begin. You will see a variety of techniques here, all designed to get you started on the path to chili perfection. Chili is not an exact science however. It is a way to express your culinary self!

REAL TEXAS CHILI

An easy and authentic "bowl of red" using a commercial chile blend.

2 tablespoons (29 ml) vegetable oil
3 pounds (1.36 kg) boneless beef chuck, cut into inch cubes
1 large onion, chopped
3 cloves garlic, minced
2 teaspoons (6 g) masa harina
3 tablespoons (22 g) Pendery's Original Chile Blend
1 tablespoon (6 g) ground roasted cumin
1 tablespoon (4 g) dried Mexican oregano
3 cups (.7 L) beef stock
1 cup (250 ml) tomato puree
1½ teaspoon (7.5 g) salt
A few grinds of black peppercorns
½ teaspoon (2 g) cayenne

Place oil in a heavy-bottomed pot and sauté the beef until it is evenly cooked but not brown. Add the onion and sauté until softened. Add garlic and masa harina, stirring for about a minute. Add chile blend, cumin, oregano, beef stock, tomato puree, salt, and peppers. Bring to a boil, and then reduce heat and simmer for about 2 hours, stirring and tasting occasionally. During the last half hour, adjust seasonings to your taste.

REAL TEXAS CHILI 2

This simple, authentic chili is made using reconstituted chiles. Mix the chiles of your choice to get just the right heat.

3 pounds (1.36 kg) boneless beef chuck roast
Water
2 tablespoons (29 ml) oil
2 cups (473 ml) beef stock
1 cup (250 ml) tomato puree
8 dried red chiles, reconstituted and ground into paste
4 cloves of garlic, diced
1 tablespoon (4 g) dried Mexican oregano
1½ teaspoon (7.5 g) salt

Place whole roast in large heavy-bottomed pot and cover with water. Bring to a boil, then reduce heat and simmer for 2–3 hours, until tender. Remove beef and drain water. Set beef aside to cool slightly.

Using two forks, pull the beef into bite-sized pieces. Place oil in pot and heat. Add beef pieces to oil and sauté briefly. Add the beef stock, pureed tomatoes, chile paste, garlic, oregano, and salt to the pot and simmer for 30 minutes.

GARDEN FRESH TEXAS CHILI

True chili fans would say that the earthy depth of dried chiles is what gives it authentic flavor. But the brightness of fresh chiles, straight from the farmer's market, makes this chili sing with flavor.

8 fresh red New Mexico chiles, split and seeded
2 fresh jalapeños, split and seeded
1 large onion, quartered
3 cloves garlic, peeled
3 tablespoons (45 ml) vegetable oil
3 pounds (1.36 kg) lean ground beef
4 fresh Roma tomatoes, pureed
4 cups (.95 L) beef stock
1 tablespoon (6 g) ground cumin
1 tablespoon (4 g) Mexican oregano
1 teaspoon (5 g) salt

Place chiles, onions, and garlic into a food processor and process into a fine dice. Heat the oil in a large saucepan and sauté the chiles, onion, and garlic until the onions are translucent and the chiles are tender. Add the ground beef, stirring and crumbling the beef until it is fully incorporated into the vegetables. Add beef stock, tomatoes, cumin, oregano, and salt. Simmer for 2–3 hours.

PURE-HEARTED CHILI

A version some purists insist on—no tomatoes are allowed to sully the pure flavor and heat of the chile peppers. Serve over rice for a home-style Texas supper.

1 tablespoon (15 ml) vegetable oil
3 pounds (1.36 kg) coarsely ground chuck
1 large onion, chopped
3 cloves garlic, minced
2 fresh jalapeños, seeded and diced
¼ cup (60 g) Pendrey's New Mexico Light chile blend
½ teaspoon (2.5 g) salt
1-2 cups (473 ml) beef stock

Place oil in a heavy-bottomed pot and add ground beef. Sauté until crumbled and evenly browned. Add onion, garlic, and fresh jalapeños and cook until onions are translucent. Add seasonings and 1 cup (237 ml) beef stock, stirring to incorporate. Simmer on low for 1–2 hours, adding beef stock as needed to keep moist. Taste, adjust salt, and remove from heat. Place overnight in refrigerator. Before serving, skim any fat from the top before reheating.

TRADITIONAL NEW MEXICO RED CHILI

Traditional New Mexico chiles are built around pork rather than beef. I love the sweetness of the pork combined with the smoky gentleness of New Mexican chili powder. New Mexico chiles are warm, but not too hot, creating a gentle bowl of goodness that is perfect accompanied alongside refried or stewed beans. Blanch the garlic before using to create a gentler garlic flavor.

Vegetable oil
3 pounds (1.36 kg) pork shoulder, fat trimmed and cut into 1″ chunks
2 medium white onions, chopped
6 cloves garlic, peeled, blanched and minced
1 tablespoon (9.5 g) masa harina
1 cup (120 g) ground dried New Mexican red chili powder
2 teaspoons (3 g) dried Mexican oregano
1 teaspoon (2 g) roasted ground cumin
4 cups (.95 L) blend of beef and chicken stock

Place 2 tablespoons (29 ml) oil in a large heavy-bottomed pot and heat it gently. Add a single layer of pork chunks and brown them gently on all sides. Repeat in small batches until all pork is cooked. Set aside pork and pan juices.

Place 2 tablespoons (29 ml) oil in the pot, and add onions and garlic. Sauté gently until softened, about 5 minutes. Sprinkle in the masa harina and stir for 2 or 3 minutes. Add chili powder, oregano, and cumin and 4 cups (.95 L) of broth. Bring to a boil, stirring to incorporate seasonings. Remove sauce from heat and set aside to cool slightly. When cool enough to work with, place sauce in a food processor and puree to a smooth consistency. Return the sauce to the pot and add reserved pork and pan juices. Bring to a boil, and then reduce to a low simmer for about two hours or until meat is very tender.

TRADITIONAL NEW MEXICO GREEN CHILI

A fresh-tasting celebration of green chiles; this is a good place to experiment with the milder fresh chile varieties. For added heat, swirl pureed jalapeños in during the last half hour of cooking.

8 fresh roasted and peeled Anaheim or Poblano chiles
Vegetable oil
3 pounds (1.36 kg) pork shoulder, fat trimmed and cut into 1" chunks
2 medium white onions, chopped
4–6 cloves garlic, peeled, blanched and minced
1 tablespoon (9.5 g) masa harina
1 tablespoon (4 g) dried Mexican oregano
3–4 cups (700–950 ml) chicken stock
Salt
1–2 fresh jalapeños, pureed

Roast fresh, whole green chiles by placing them on a hot grill, turning with tongs until they are charred on all sides. When they are cool, rub the blackened peel off and rinse. Remove stems, cut in half lengthwise, remove seeds, and dice. Set aside.

Place 2 tablespoons (30 ml) oil in a large heavy-bottomed pot and heat it gently. Add a single layer of pork chunks and brown them gently on all sides. Repeat in small batches until all pork is cooked. Set aside pork and pan juices.

Add onions and garlic to the pot. Sauté gently until softened, about 5 minutes. Sprinkle in the masa harina and stir for 2 or 3 minutes. Add the pork and juices back into the pot, along with the chiles and oregano. Cover pork with stock, bring to a boil, and then reduce and simmer for 2 hours. If you like a spicier chili, spoon in a swirl of fresh pureed jalapeño during the last half hour. Adjust salt as needed in the last 10 minutes. Serve with fresh, warm homemade flour tortillas; recipe in Chapter 9.

CLASSIC HOME-STYLE CHILI

Unless you grew up in Texas or the southwestern US, this is the chili recipe you probably grew up with—a combination of ground beef, chili powder, tomatoes, and beans. A mild and most basic version—use it as a springboard to create your own special recipe!

1 tablespoon (15 ml) vegetable oil
3 pounds (1.36 kg) lean ground beef
1 large onion, diced
1 medium green pepper, diced
2 cloves garlic
4 cups (1 L) tomato puree
2 cups (500 ml) beef stock
¼ cup (30 g) chili powder
2 teaspoons (6 g) cumin
1 teaspoon (2 g) Mexican oregano
1 teaspoon (5 g) salt
2-15 ounce (445 ml) cans kidney beans,
    drained and rinsed

Sauté ground beef in oil until evenly browned. Drain excess oil and place back on heat. Add onions, peppers, and garlic, cooking until softened, about 5 minutes. Add tomato puree, beef stock, chili powder, cumin, oregano, and salt. Bring to a boil, and then reduce heat and simmer for 2–3 hours. During the last half hour of cooking, add beans.

Serve topped with shredded cheddar cheese and chopped onions, and with tortilla chips or soda crackers on the side.

REAL CINCINNATI CHILI

Traditional? Well, it is in Cincinnati where the dish was popularized. Proponents of this cinnamon-spiced chili, traditionally served over spaghetti noodles, call its flavor positively addictive. The meat is boiled rather than browned to achieve its distinctive smooth texture. Make it a day ahead to give the seasonings a chance to fully develop.

2 pounds (907 g) ground beef
4 cups (946 ml) beef stock
2 cups (500 ml) tomato puree
2 yellow onions, diced
1 tablespoon (15 ml) Worcestershire sauce
2 tablespoons (14 g) unsweetened cocoa
¼ cup (30 g) chili powder
1 teaspoon (2.5 g) cinnamon
1 teaspoon (2.5 g) ground cumin
¼ teaspoon (.5 g) ground cloves
1 whole bay leaf
2 tablespoons (30 ml) cider vinegar
Salt

Place ground beef and stock into a large heavy-bottomed pot. Cook and stir over medium heat until ground beef is in very small crumbles and cooked through. Simmer for 30 minutes. Add diced onions and all seasonings into the pot. Bring to a boil, then turn down heat and simmer on low for 3–4 hours, adjusting liquid if it becomes too thick. Adjust salt as desired, depending on the salt content of stock and tomatoes.

Remove from heat, cool at room temperature, and then refrigerate overnight. Before serving, skim any fat from the top before reheating.

Toppings are a key component of Cincinnati chili; make a "five-way" by serving over spaghetti noodles and topping with cheese, onions, and kidney beans. My favorite way to eat this chili is over hot dogs.
cooked spaghetti
mild shredded cheddar cheese
diced white onions
cooked kidney beans

WHITE CHILI

Although chili made with chicken and white beans is not strictly traditional, I have included it here because it has so many fans.

1 pound (450 g) navy or Great Northern beans, soaked overnight, drained and rinsed
6 cups (1.4 L) chicken stock
8 fresh roasted and peeled Anaheim or Poblano chiles
1 tablespoon (15 ml) vegetable oil
1 medium onion, chopped
2 cloves garlic, blanched and minced
2–3 jalapeños, chopped
¼ cup (30 g) Pendery's White Chile Blend
4 cups (918 g) diced cooked chicken
Salt to taste
Sour cream
Fresh chopped cilantro

Combine pre-soaked beans and chicken stock in a large heavy-bottomed pot and bring to a boil. Reduce heat and simmer about 2 hours.

Roast fresh whole green chiles by placing them on a hot grill, turning with tongs until they are charred on all sides. When they are cool, rub the blackened peel off and rinse. Remove stems, cut in half lengthwise, remove seeds, and dice. Set aside.

In a separate skillet, sauté onion, garlic, and jalapeño in oil until tender. Add in green chiles and all seasonings, stirring to incorporate. Transfer seasoned mix into the bean mixture with chicken. Bring to a boil, and then reduce heat and simmer for 30 minutes. Taste and salt before serving.

Serve topped with sour cream and a garnish of chopped cilantro.

Home-style Chili

In competition, home-style chili is defined as any combination of ingredients that is seasoned with chile peppers. This is indeed a broad definition, designed to unleash the creative spirit of the home chef.

In practice, home-style chili is a matter of family traditions—the perfect bowl of chili for the football game, the pot simmering on the stove after a day of skiing, the comfort of a warm bowl in front of a cozy fire. For our family, our most special chili recipe goes hand in hand with football. It is not a Sunday in autumn unless there is a pot bubbling away on the stove. Green Bay Packer Chili is a closely guarded secret in our house—so secret, in fact, that it is not even included in this book. But we do occasionally engage in a chili challenge on game day!

Chili variations range from subtle tweaks to the traditional tomato-based bowl to those highlighting white and green chiles or vegetable, nut and bean ingredients. The only true requirement is the chile pepper itself. Whether your family prefers the mildness of blended chili powders, the zing of ground chiles or the intense rush of fresh hot chiles, there is one simple truth: it's all chili!

BARTENDER'S CHILI

Got a cooler full of cold ones? Create a flavor bridge by adding beer to the pot, then serving the same beer with dinner. I like a dark stout in this recipe, but some say any beer will suffice. My friend Martha Greenlaw always adds dark rum too. I have taken up her habit—using a special Newfoundland rum called Screech.

1 tablespoon (15 ml) vegetable oil
3 pounds (1.36 kg) ground beef
1 large onion, coarsely chopped
2 red or yellow bell peppers, seeded, coarsely chopped
1 large jalapeño, chopped
2 cloves garlic, peeled and sliced
1-28 ounce (300 g) can crushed tomatoes
8 ounces (236 ml) tomato sauce
2 tablespoons (15 g) chili powder
¼ teaspoon (.5 g) cayenne pepper
1 tablespoon (12 g) sugar
1 tablespoon (12 g) salt
1-12 ounce (355 ml) bottle Guinness or other stout
½ cup (236 ml) dark rum
2-15 ounce (300 g) cans black beans, drained and rinsed
Salt and pepper to taste
Green onions, chopped
Cheddar cheese, grated

Brown ground beef with oil in Dutch oven. Add onion, bell peppers, jalapeño, and garlic, and continue to cook, stirring occasionally until vegetables are tender. Add crushed tomatoes, tomato sauce, chili powder, cayenne, sugar, salt, beer, and rum. Simmer two hours. Drain black beans and rinse to remove excess starch. Add to the pot and continue to cook for 20 minutes to heat beans thoroughly. Adjust seasonings as needed. Garnish with grated cheddar cheese and chopped green onions.

GRILLED SAUSAGE AND PEPPERS CHILI

Game-night chili for the guys—like a spicy sausage and pepper hoagie in a bowl!

2 pounds (907 g) hot Italian sausage, grilled and cut into ½-inch pieces
Olive oil
2 large red or yellow bell peppers, cut into thick slices
1 large onion, cut into thick slices and grilled
1 whole head of garlic
3 tablespoons (18 g) chili powder
1 teaspoon (2 g) roasted ground cumin
1 teaspoon (2 g) dried Mexican oregano
½ teaspoon (1 g) cayenne
1-12 ounce (354 ml) bottle beer
2 cups (322 g) crushed tomatoes
3 tablespoons (45 ml) tomato paste
2 cups (300 g) cooked kidney beans, drained and rinsed
1 tablespoon (9.5 g) masa harina, optional

Do ahead: Drizzle oil over garlic head, wrap in foil, and place on grill. Place sausages on hot grill, cooking on all sides until browned and cooked through. Toss thick rings of onion and peppers in olive oil and add to grill, turning until caramelized and soft. Remove sausages from grill and cut into ½" chunks. Remove peppers and onions from grill and chop coarsely. Open foil pack and remove garlic. Pull out cloves and squeeze garlic pulp into a small bowl. Set sausage and vegetables aside until ready to use.

To assemble chili: Place cooked sausages, peppers, onions, and garlic in a large, heavy-bottomed pot, and add seasonings, stirring to coat. Stir in beer, and add tomatoes, paste, and beans. Bring to a boil, and then turn to low heat to simmer for an hour or until sauce has thickened. (If needed, sprinkle in masa harina and stir until sauce thickens.)

Serve in hollowed-out bread boules, and top with shredded cheese and chopped white onions.

"MAKE MINE A DOUBLE" CHILI

A friend once asked: But can you make it with Scotch? I went him one better, and added both a big splash of blended Scotch whiskey and a Scotch bonnet pepper. The resulting spicy bowl answered his question.

2 tablespoons (30 ml) vegetable oil
1 large onion, chopped
1 red bell pepper, chopped
2 cloves garlic, minced
1 Scotch bonnet pepper, stemmed, seeded, and minced
3 pounds (1300 g) ground beef
3 tablespoons (18 g) chili powder
½ teaspoon (2 g) garlic powder
1 teaspoon (2 g) Mexican oregano
½ teaspoon (2.5 g) salt
2 tablespoons (30 ml) molasses
1-29 ounce can diced tomatoes
½ cup (120 ml) Scotch whiskey
1 cup (250 ml) beef stock

Place oil in a heavy-bottomed pot and add onions and pepper. Sauté until softened, and then add the Scotch bonnet. Stir in ground beef and cook until crumbled. Add chili powder, garlic, oregano, molasses, tomatoes, and Scotch. Reduce to a simmer and cook for one hour.

FIVE ALARM CHILI

One alarm for every type of chile pepper in the pot—proceed with caution!

½ pound (225 g) bacon
2 pounds (907 g) ground chuck
1 pound (450 g) ground pork
1 green bell pepper, diced
1 yellow onion, diced
2 cloves garlic, minced
6 jalapeño peppers, seeded and chopped
6 habanero peppers, seeded and chopped
8 red Anaheim peppers, seeded and diced
1 tablespoon (4 g) crushed red pepper flakes
3 tablespoons (18 g) ancho chili powder
1 tablespoon (4 g) ground cumin
2 cups (473 ml) beef stock
1-12 (354 ml) ounce can beer
1-28 ounce (563 g) can crushed tomatoes
1-28 ounce (563 g) can whole peeled tomatoes, drained
3 ounces (88 ml) tomato paste
4 cups (900 g) cooked pinto beans, rinsed and drained

Cook bacon in a large heavy-bottomed stockpot. Drain excess grease and set aside bacon. Add beef and pork, stirring to crumble and evenly cook. Stir in green pepper, onion, garlic, jalapeño peppers, habanero peppers, Anaheim peppers, and spices. Add beef stock, beer, and all tomatoes.

Bring to a boil, and then reduce heat and simmer uncovered for 2 hours, stirring occasionally. Chop bacon and add it back to the pot. Stir in beans 30 minutes before serving.

ANDRE'S FLEMISH CHILI WITH FRITES

¼ cup (60 ml) olive oil

4 tablespoons (60 g) of butter

2 pounds (900 g) of stewing beef cut into 1″ cubes

1 sweet onion, chopped small

1 red bell pepper, chopped small

1 green bell pepper, chopped small

2 stalks celery, medium chop

¼ cup (31 g) banana peppers, chopped small

3 cloves garlic, chopped fine

1-12 ounce (350 g) can tomato paste

4 tablespoons (60 ml) hot vinegar—from a jar of hot peppers or pickles

1 tablespoon (4 g) cumin

4 bay leaves

1 teaspoon (5 g) salt

1 tablespoon (15 ml) Worcestershire sauce

1 tablespoon (15 ml) hot sauce

1-12 ounce (350 g) bottle light ale

2–3 tablespoons (30 - 50 g) sour cream

1-15 ounce (425 g) can red kidney beans, rinsed and drained

Place pan over high heat and get it very hot. Place the olive oil and butter in the pan and quickly sear the beef in batches. Set the seared beef aside. Add the onions to pan and sauté. When onions are caramelized, add the peppers, celery and banana peppers. Cook about 3 minutes, and then add garlic. Cook another 2 minutes. Add all ingredients except sour cream and beans. Simmer for about 2 hours. Stir in sour cream and beans and continue to simmer for about 30 minutes.

FRITES

6 russet potatoes, sliced like steak fries
Lard, melted or vegetable, canola, or peanut oil—or a combo

Soak the sliced potatoes in ice water 1–8 hours. Dry potatoes in batches using a salad spinner.

Dry those again using cotton towel. Fry potatoes in batches at 320 degrees until tiny little bubbles or blisters appear on potatoes.

Put potatoes on wire rack to cool for at least an hour—the cooler they are the better they will be after the second fry. Fry again in batches at 375 degrees until golden.

Drain fries and place on serving plate. Serve chili over fries and garnish with garlic mayo.

GARLIC MAYO

1 cup Hellman's mayo
6 very fresh cloves of garlic
Zest from ½ large lemon
Juice from ½ large lemon
¼ t fresh ground black pepper
½ t salt

Mix in food processor until very smooth. Chill at least 2 hours.

TRINITY CHILI

Inspired by mole sauces which incorporate three traditional chile flavors; chocolate is added to the chili at the last minute to richen the sauce and round out the rough edges.

2 tablespoons (30 ml) vegetable oil
2 pounds (907 g) lean ground beef
1 pound (453 g) ground pork
1 large onion, chopped
3 cloves of garlic, minced
2-28 ounce (1.1 L) cans crushed tomatoes
2 tablespoons (12 g) ground ancho chili powder
2 tablespoons (12 g) ground mulatto chili powder
2 tablespoons (12 g) ground pasilla negro chili powder
3 teaspoons (7.5 g) roasted ground cumin
1 teaspoon (2.5 g) Mexican oregano
2 teaspoons (10 g) salt
2 bay leaves
2 ounce (57 g) solid bittersweet chocolate

Heat oil in a heavy-bottomed pan. Place beef and pork in pot, stirring and breaking into fine crumbles. When meat is evenly cooked, add chopped onions and garlic, sautéing until onions are tender. Stir in tomatoes, ground chiles, cumin, oregano, salt, and bay leaves. Bring to a boil, and then reduce heat to low and simmer for 2 hours. Before serving, remove bay leaves and add chocolate. Stir to melt, and simmer another 10 minutes or so. Refrigerate overnight. The next day, skim fat from the top, reheat, and serve with refried beans on the side.

BETH'S COLORADO BEANLESS CHILI

My friends Beth and Dargan prefer their chili hot and beanless. If you are making chili for the whole family, don't add jalapeños to the pot. You can float strips of jalapeño or a swirl of pureed jalapeño in the adults' bowls.

Vegetable oil
Salt and pepper
1 pound (680 g) chuck steak, cut into 1–2" pieces
3-15 oz (1.875 L) cans petite cut tomatoes
1-15 oz (625 ml) can fire-roasted, canned, chopped tomatoes
1 red bell pepper, chopped
1 green bell pepper, chopped
1 large sweet white onion, chopped
2 cloves of garlic, minced
2 teaspoons (5 g) ground cumin
1 teaspoon (3 g) Mexican oregano
3 tablespoons (18 g) good chili powder
1 teaspoon (5 g) brown sugar
6–10 sliced jalapeños

Generously salt and pepper the beef chunks. Heat oil in skillet and add seasoned beef, sautéing until light brown. Place the meat and all the juices into a crock pot. In the same skillet, sauté chopped peppers, onion, and garlic in olive oil until soft. Add these to crock pot. Add the 4 cans of tomatoes, brown sugar, and seasonings. Stir to mix ingredients and simmer on low for eight hours. After about four hours, check seasoning and adjust according to taste. If you are incorporating jalapeños into the chili, add them now and simmer another 30 minutes.

Top with your choice of sliced jalapeños, shredded cheddar cheese, and chopped chives. Serve with large tortilla chips for scooping.

DUTCH OVEN CHILI

A spicy and delicious oven recipe, made extra-special with a topping of cornbread biscuits.

4 tablespoons (57 g) butter
3 large onions, chopped
4 cloves garlic, minced
1 large green bell pepper, chopped
2 pounds (907 g) lean ground beef
1 pound (453 g) pork sausage
2 cups crushed tomatoes
1 teaspoon (7 g) honey
1 bay leaf
3 tablespoons (18 g) mild ground chile paste (about 3 dry New Mexico chiles, reconstituted and ground)
1 tablespoon (6 g) ground New Mexican ancho powder
1 teaspoon (2.5 g) cumin
½ teaspoon (1 g) cinnamon
3 fresh jalapeño peppers, stemmed, seeded, and diced
1 cup (236 ml) dry red wine
1 cup (236 ml) strong coffee
2 teaspoons (10 g) salt
3–4 cups (900 g) cooked pinto or black beans (two 15 ounce (900 g) cans, rinsed and drained)
Cornbread Topper:
1 cup (99 g) all-purpose flour
1 cup (170 g) cornmeal
2 teaspoons baking powder
¼ teaspoon (1.25 g) salt
1 egg
½ cup (118 ml) milk
½ cup (130 ml) sour cream

HOME-STYLE CHILI

Melt butter in a large heavy-bottomed pan. Add the onions, garlic, and bell pepper, cooking until softened. Add the ground meats, stirring until broken into crumbles and evenly cooked. Stir in the tomatoes, honey, and bay leaf.

Place ground meat mixture in large Dutch oven. Add the rest of the seasonings, jalapeños, wine, coffee, and salt. Place in 300 degree oven, cover, and bake for about 3 hours. Stir beans into the chili, and bake for another half hour.

To add a cornbread topper, increase heat to 400 degrees. Mix dry ingredients together in a bowl. Blend egg into mixture with a fork. Add milk and sour cream, mixing just until thoroughly incorporated. Remove cover from Dutch oven and drop cornbread batter in large spoonfuls onto hot chili. Bake uncovered for 15 minutes. Biscuits should be lightly browned and cooked through.

MEATBALL CHILI

I love meatballs and will use almost any excuse to make them. These small chili-flavored meat-balls in a chunky vegetable sauce are great served over Mexican rice.

Chili Sauce:
2 tablespoons (30 ml) vegetable oil
1 large onion, chopped
2 cloves garlic, minced
1 carrot, peeled and chopped
1 stalk celery, chopped
1 large red bell pepper, seeded and chopped
2 tablespoons (30) chipotles in adobo, diced
3 tablespoons (18 g) chili powder
1 teaspoon (2.5 g) roasted ground cumin
1 tablespoon (5 g) sugar
1 teaspoon (2.5 g) Mexican oregano
1-28 ounce (833 ml) can diced tomatoes
2 cups (473 ml) beef stock

Meatballs:
1 pound (453 g) ground beef
1 pound (453 g) ground pork
1 small onion, diced
2 cloves garlic, minced
2 eggs
1 cup (59 g) bread crumbs
¼ cup (236 ml) milk
1 teaspoon (2 g) chili powder
1 teaspoon (3 g) Mexican oregano
1 teaspoon (5 g) salt
½ teaspoon (2.5 g) black pepper

HOME-STYLE CHILI

Heat oil in a large heavy-bottomed pot. Sauté onions, garlic, carrot, celery, and pepper until vegetables are softened. Add chipotles and all seasonings. Stir in tomatoes and beef stock. Bring to a boil, reduce heat, and simmer while you assemble meatballs.

Mix all meatball ingredients in a bowl, adjusting milk and breadcrumbs to get a firm consistency. Form small meatballs and place on a cookie sheet. Place meatballs in a preheated 350 degree oven and bake, turning as needed, until they are cooked through. Remove meatballs from cookie sheet and place into simmering chili sauce. Simmer for 45 minutes to an hour. Serve chili sauce and meatballs over Mexican rice with a side of Fried Corn.

CHILI WITH APPLES AND RAISINS

The rich undercurrent of fruit and sweet spices make a delicious and unusual combination. I use leftover chili from this recipe to make tamale pie.

¼ cup (35 g) raisins
1 cup (236 ml) strong coffee
1 tablespoon (15 ml) vegetable oil
2 pounds (907 g) ground beef
1 large white onion, chopped
1 red bell pepper, chopped
1 clove garlic, minced
1-28 ounce (563 g) can crushed tomatoes
1-6 ounce (180 ml) can tomato paste
1 ½ cups (354 ml) beef stock
2 large red apples, peeled and chopped
½ cup (57 g) slivered almonds
3 tablespoons (18 g) mild chili powder
2 tablespoons (12 g) cocoa powder
1 tablespoon (6 g) ground cinnamon
1 teaspoon (5 g) salt
1-15 ounce (450 g) can black beans, drained and rinsed

Soak raisins in coffee for 15 minutes or until plumped.

Place vegetable oil in a large heavy-bottomed pot. Add onions, pepper, and garlic, and sauté until softened. Add ground beef, cooking and stirring until beef is evenly cooked and in small crumbles. Stir in raisins, coffee, tomatoes, tomato paste, stock, apples, almonds, cocoa, and seasonings. Bring to a boil, and then reduce heat to simmer for about an hour. Add beans and continue to cook for another 15 minutes, or until beans are heated through.

CAJUN CHILI

My mom's recipe—with the requisite Holy Trinity—a mirepoix of onions, bell pepper, and celery. Cayenne and Louisiana hot sauce provide the punch. Serve with soda crackers.

3 tablespoons (45 ml) vegetable oil
1 large yellow onion, chopped
1 large green bell pepper, chopped
3 stalks celery, chopped
3 cloves garlic, minced
2 pounds (907 kg) ground beef
2 tablespoons (12 g) chili powder
2 teaspoons (6 g) cumin
1 teaspoon (2.5 g) Mexican oregano
4 tablespoons Louisiana hot sauce
1 tablespoon (6 g) cayenne pepper
3 cups (709 ml) beef stock
1-28 ounce (830 ml) can crushed tomatoes
1-8 ounce (236 ml) can tomato sauce
Green onions

Place oil in a heavy-bottomed pot. Sauté onions, bell pepper, celery, and garlic until vegetables are softened. Add the ground beef, breaking and stirring until evenly cooked. Add all seasonings, beef stock, and tomatoes. Bring to a boil, and then reduce and simmer uncovered for 1 hour. Serve topped with chopped green onions.

RED-EYE CHILI

Traditional red-eye gravy relies on salty country ham and coffee for its flavor, and the combo works well as a southern-style chili base. For an authentic southern tailgate party, pair this chili with miniature ham biscuits.

2 tablespoons (30 ml) vegetable oil
¼ pound (113 g) Virginia country ham, diced
1 large onion, coarsely chopped
2 garlic cloves, blanched and minced
3 pounds (1.36 kg) ground beef
¼ cup (30 g) ground ancho chili
2 teaspoons (6 g) roasted ground cumin
1 teaspoon (2.5 g) Mexican oregano
1-12 ounce (354 ml) bottle beer
1 cup (236 ml) strong black coffee
1-6 ounce (180 ml) can tomato paste
1 tablespoon (15 ml) molasses

Place oil in heavy-bottomed pot and fry ham. Add onion and garlic, sautéing until onion is softened. Add ground beef and stir until crumbled and evenly cooked. Stir in seasonings. Pour in beer, stirring until foam has disappeared. Add coffee, tomato paste, and molasses. Bring to a boil, and then reduce to simmer for about an hour.

CHILI DOG CHILI

The texture of chili for dogs and burgers should be smoother than that of regular chili, and thick enough to serve as a topping. We boil the ground beef rather than sautéing it to achieve a smaller crumble, and thicken with corn flour to achieve rich gravy.

2 pounds (907 g) lean ground beef
1 onion, finely chopped
2 medium garlic cloves, minced
¼ cup (30 g) chili powder
1 teaspoon (3 g) ground cumin
2 teaspoons (10 g) sugar
¼ cup (65 ml) tomato paste
2 cups (473 ml) beef stock
4 tablespoons (19 g) masa harina
2 teaspoons (10 g) salt

Place ground beef in a heavy-bottomed pot and add one cup of beef stock. Boil and stir until the meat is broken into even crumbles and cooked through. Add onion and garlic, simmering until onion is translucent. Add chili powder, cumin, and sugar and stir into the meat mixture to incorporate. Stir in tomato paste and stock. Add masa harina to thicken. Bring chili to a boil, and then reduce heat to low and simmer until very thick, about 30 minutes.

Grill hot dogs or hamburger patties, and toast buns. Add heaping spoonfuls and garnish with shredded cheese, chopped onions, beans, or jalapeños.

CHILI FOR A CROWD

A big, big pot of classic chili—enough for about 25 hungry people.

4 tablespoons (60 ml) vegetable oil
10 medium onions, chopped
6 cloves garlic, minced
6 pounds (2.75 kg) ground beef
½ cup (60 g) chili powder
2 teaspoons (5 g) Mexican oregano
2 teaspoons (6 g) ground cumin
2 teaspoons (10 g) salt
2 teaspoons (6 g) cayenne
2 teaspoons Tabasco sauce
4-28 ounce (3.3 L) cans crushed tomatoes
2-6 ounce (254 ml) cans tomato paste
1 cup (236 ml) beef stock
6-12 ounce (2.05 kg) cans kidney beans, drained and rinsed

Sauté onions in oil until softened. Add garlic and cook briefly. Add ground beef and all seasonings, stirring until broken up and evenly cooked. Add tomatoes, paste, and stock. Simmer uncovered for about an hour, adding stock if needed to maintain consistency. Add beans during the last 15 minutes of cooking to heat through. Serve with corn chips.

GRINGO'S GARDEN CHILI VERDE

Tomatillos, jalapeños, and onions are core ingredients in our summer garden, so this chili is a big favorite at harvest time. If you use commercial green salsa in this recipe, add an extra jalapeño to the pot for a little more kick.

4 tablespoons (60 ml) oil
3 pounds (1.36 kg) lean pork shoulder, cut into half-inch (1.25 cm) cubes
1 large white onion, chopped
4 cloves garlic, minced
1 jalapeño, chopped (optional)
2–3 cups (300–450 g) green salsa (store-bought or from recipe in Chapter 7)
1-12 ounce (354 ml) bottle of Mexican beer, such as Corona (use chicken stock if you prefer)
Salt and pepper to taste
Sour cream

Heat oil in 10″ (25.4 cm) Dutch oven. Season cubed pork with salt and pepper and add to pot, stirring until meat is well browned. Add onion, garlic, and jalapeño to the pot, and sauté until vegetables are tender. Add green salsa and beer, and season to taste. Simmer for 2 hours. Serve with a dollop of sour cream.

CHRISTMAS CHILI

In New Mexico they ask "green or red"? To get both, the correct reply is "Christmas." This is the way my husband likes his pork chili—a green chile base with a swirl of red chile sauce on top.

1 tablespoon (15 ml) vegetable oil
3 pounds (1.36 kg) ground pork
1 bunch of green onions, whites and greens chopped
3 Anaheim chiles, peeled, seeded and chopped
¼ cup (30 g) green chili powder
1 tablespoon (5 g) ground cumin
1 tablespoon (6 g) crushed green chili
4 cups (946 ml) chicken stock
3 cups (709 ml) crushed tomatoes
2 cups (325 g) cooked pinto beans (or 1-15 ounce can, drained and rinsed)
½ teaspoon (2.5 g) salt

Red chile sauce
Sour cream

Place oil in a large heavy-bottomed pot and sauté the ground pork until it is evenly cooked. Add onions, chilies, green chili powder, cumin, and crushed green chili, stirring to coat pork. Add stock and tomatoes. Bring to a boil, and then turn heat to low and simmer for 1 hour. Add beans and simmer another 15 minutes or until beans are heated through. Serve with a swirl of red chile sauce and a dollop of sour cream.

VIRGINIA PEANUT CHILI WITH PORK

Here in Virginia, our hand-cooked peanuts are large and flavorful, with a crispness that is hard to match in regular grocery store peanuts. They add sweetness and body to the chili, pairing beautifully with the delicate taste of the pork.

2 tablespoons (30 ml) vegetable oil

1 medium onion, diced

3 cloves garlic, minced

1½ cups (225 g) roasted, unsalted peanuts

1-28 ounce (828 ml) canned crushed tomatoes

1 cup (236 ml) chicken stock

2 tablespoons (12 g) ground ancho chili powder

1 teaspoon (3 g) ground coriander

1 teaspoon (3 g) ground cumin

1 teaspoon (5 g) salt

1 tablespoon honey

2 tablespoons (30 ml) vegetable oil

2 pounds (907 g) pork tenderloin, cut into 1" chunks

1 tablespoon (6 g) chili blend

Heat oil in a large heavy-bottomed pot. Add onion and garlic, and sauté until onion is translucent. Stir in peanuts, tomatoes, stock, seasonings, and honey. Bring to a boil, and then reduce to low heat and simmer for 30 minutes.

While the sauce is simmering, place oil in a large skillet. Season pork chunks with chili blend and sauté until fully cooked. Stir the pork into the peanut and chili sauce. Simmer until pork is tender. Taste and adjust seasonings. To serve, garnish with chopped scallion tops and chopped roasted peanuts.

NEW MEXICO ROASTED GREEN CHILE STEW

Fresh-from-the-garden ingredients and home-roasted peppers make this mild summertime stew extra-special.

2 pounds (907 g) green Anaheim or New Mexico chiles

2 tablespoons (30 ml) vegetable oil

1 pound (453 g) pork shoulder, fat trimmed and cubed

3 cloves garlic, chopped

1 large onion, chopped

1 teaspoon (3 g) ground cumin

1 teaspoon (2.5 g) dried Mexican oregano

2 cups (472 ml) chicken stock

1 jalapeño pepper, diced

10–12 small new red potatoes, scrubbed and cubed

4 Roma tomatoes, pureed

salt

Roast fresh, whole green chiles by placing them on a hot grill, turning with tongs until they are charred on all sides. When they are cool, rub the blackened peel off and rinse. Remove stems, cut in half lengthwise, remove seeds, and dice. Set aside.

Place 2 tablespoons (30 ml) oil in a large heavy-bottomed pot. Add pork and brown gently on all sides. Add onions and garlic and sauté gently until softened, about 5 minutes. Add cumin, oregano, and chicken stock. Reduce the heat to low and simmer for about 30 minutes.

Add potatoes and simmer until the potatoes are nearly tender. Add diced roasted peppers, jalapeño, and pureed tomatoes. Simmer on low for 30 minutes to incorporate flavors.

HOGWASH CHILI

A dark, bold, and mysterious chili. Try the chili rib version!

2 tablespoons (30 ml) vegetable oil

1 large onion, diced

3 cloves garlic, minced

2 jalapeños, seeded and diced

3 pounds (1.36 kg) ground pork

1-28 ounce (833 ml) can pureed tomatoes

2 cups (472 ml) beef stock

1 cup (236 ml) water

2 tablespoons (12 g) ancho chili powder

1 tablespoon (6 g) chipotle chili powder

1 tablespoon (3 g) instant espresso

1 tablespoon (4 g) dark cocoa powder

1 tablespoon (5 g) cinnamon

2 tablespoons (14 g) brown sugar

1 teaspoon (5 g) salt

2 cups (330 g) cooked black beans, rinsed and drained

Place oil in a heavy-bottomed pot. Sauté onions, garlic, and jalapeño until softened. Add ground pork and stir until broken into crumbles and evenly cooked. Stir in tomatoes, beef stock, water, and seasonings. Bring to a boil. Reduce heat and simmer for one hour. Add black beans and cook until heated through. Garnish with chopped green onions.

Variation: Hogwash Chili Ribs

Make sauce without meat and beans. Simmer for 30 minutes. While the sauce is simmering, salt and pepper 4–6 pounds (1.8–2.7 kg) of baby back ribs. Place in shallow roasting pan and brown 15 minutes on each side. Remove from fat and place in large crock pot. Pour sauce over ribs, turning to coat. Cover and cook on low for 8 hours or until tender.

PUMPKIN CHILI

A soothing autumn bowl of comfort. Serve in small hollowed-out pumpkins for a Halloween night supper.

2 tablespoons (30 ml) olive oil
1 onion, chopped
1 large red bell pepper, chopped
2 cloves garlic, minced
2 pounds (900 g) ground beef
2 tablespoons (12 g) ancho chili powder
1 teaspoon (1.5 g) cinnamon
1-29 ounce (820 g) can diced tomatoes
1-15 ounce (425 g) can tomato sauce
1-15 ounce (425 g) can pumpkin puree
1 cup (250 ml) beef stock
1-15 ounce (425 g) can black beans, rinsed and drained

Place oil in heavy-bottomed pot. Add in onions, pepper, and garlic, sautéing until softened. Stir in ground beef and cook until crumbled. Sprinkle in ancho powder and cinnamon, and add tomatoes, pumpkin, and beef stock. Simmer uncovered for an hour, adjusting liquids if needed. Add black beans and cook until they are heated through. Serve with cornbread.

HARVEST CHILI WITH SQUASH, SWEET CORN, AND SPINACH

All the flavors of the midsummer garden come together in this flavorful turkey chili.

2 tablespoons (30 ml) vegetable oil
1 large onion, chopped
1 red bell pepper, chopped
2 cloves garlic minced
2 jalapeño peppers, minced
1 pound (453 g) ground turkey
1 tablespoon (6 g) New Mexico chili powder
1 teaspoon (2.5 g) Mexican oregano
1 teaspoon (3 g) ground cumin
1 teaspoon (5 g) brown sugar
3 cups (483 g) fresh tomatoes, peeled, and crushed
2 cups (472 ml) chicken stock
3 cups (483 g) butternut squash, cut into 1" (2.5 cm) cubes
1 Anaheim chile, roasted, peeled, and chopped
1 cup (160 g) sweet corn, cut fresh off cob
1-15 ounce (425 g) can kidney beans
2 cups (180 g) spinach leaves, chopped

Heat oil in a heavy-bottomed pot. Sauté onion, bell pepper, garlic, and jalapeños until vegetables are softened. Add the turkey, stirring until crumbled and evenly cooked. Sprinkle in all seasonings. Add tomatoes, chicken stock, squash, chile, corn, and kidney beans. Bring to a boil, and then reduce heat and simmer until squash is tender, about 20 minutes. Stir in the spinach leaves and cooked just until wilted.

TURKEY RATATOUILLE CHILI

All the flavors of the Mediterranean classic, but with a Tex-Mex twist.

2 tablespoons (30 ml) vegetable oil
1 large onion, chopped
1 large red bell pepper, chopped
3 garlic cloves, blanched and minced
2 pounds (907 g) ground turkey
3 teaspoons (18 g) chili powder
1 teaspoon (3 g) roasted ground cumin
1 teaspoon (2.5 g) Mexican oregano
¼ teaspoon (1 g) cayenne
2 cups (472 ml) chicken stock
1 medium zucchini, scrubbed and chopped
1 eggplant, peeled and chopped
1 cup (66 g) mushrooms, sliced
1-28 ounce (828 ml) can diced tomatoes
1 -15 ounce (425 g) can cannelloni beans, drained and rinsed
Salt and pepper to taste

Place oil in a heavy-bottomed pot. Sauté onions, bell pepper, and garlic until softened. Add ground turkey and stir to cook and break into crumbles. Stir in chili powder, cumin, oregano, and cayenne. Add chicken stock, zucchini, eggplant, mushrooms, and tomatoes. Bring to a boil, and then reduce heat and simmer for 30 minutes. Add beans and simmer until beans are heated through, another 15 minutes or so. Adjust seasonings and serve.

HANNAH'S TURKEY AND THREE BEAN CHILI

2 tablespoons (30 ml) olive oil

1 medium onion, chopped

5 garlic cloves, minced

2 pounds (907 g) of ground turkey

1-15 oz (425 g) can black beans

1-15 oz (425 g) can kidney beans

1-15 oz (425 g) can cannellini beans

1–2 fresh poblano peppers, roasted and peeled

2 large (828 ml) cans crushed tomatoes

1-4 oz (110 g) can diced green chiles

4 tablespoons (24 g) chili powder

1 teaspoon (3 g) red pepper flakes (or as desired)

1½ teaspoons (7.5 g) salt

1 teaspoon (5 g) pepper

In a sauté pan, cook onions and garlic in olive oil. Add turkey and sauté until the turkey is cooked through. Place turkey, onions, and garlic in crock pot with the rest of the ingredients and simmer on low heat all day. Top with a dollop of sour cream and crumble tortilla chips on top.

SPICY CHICKEN CHILI

Chicken and white beans with a spicy tomato base.

3 tablespoons (45 ml) olive oil
2 large onions, chopped
1 large green bell pepper, chopped
3 garlic cloves, minced
2 pounds (900 g) boneless, skinless chicken breasts, cubed
3 tablespoons (18 g) chili powder
2 teaspoons (6 g) ground cumin
1 teaspoon (2.5 g) Mexican oregano
1 teaspoon (3 g) cayenne pepper
1-29 ounce (820 g) can diced tomatoes, with liquid
2½ cups (600 ml) chicken stock
2 cups (475 ml) water
1-6 ounce (170 g) can tomato paste
2-15 ounce (425 g) cans white beans, rinsed and drained

Place oil in a heavy-bottomed pot and sauté onions, peppers, and garlic until softened. Add chicken and sauté until nearly cooked through. Sprinkle chili powder, cumin, oregano, and cayenne over chicken. Stir in tomatoes, stock, water, and paste. Reduce heat and simmer about 45 minutes. Add beans and continue to cook until they are heated through, about 20 minutes.

K.D.'S WICKED WHITE CHILI

1 pound (465 g) Great Northern beans, soaked overnight in water, drained and rinsed
3 cups (709 ml) chicken stock
3 cups (709 ml) vegetable stock
6 cloves garlic, minced
2 medium yellow onions, diced
2 tablespoons (30 ml) vegetable oil
12 ounces (340 g) ground chicken sausage
2-4 ounce (227 g) cans chopped green chiles
2 jalapeño or serrano peppers, diced
2 teaspoons (6 g) ground cumin
2 teaspoons (5 g) dried Mexican oregano
¼ teaspoon (1 g) ground cloves
½ teaspoon (2 g) cayenne pepper
1 teaspoon (4 g) white pepper
2 to 3 cups (460–690 g) cooked chicken, diced
Grated cheese, chopped fresh cilantro, chopped scallions

Combine beans, stocks, 5 cloves of garlic, and half the onions in a large chili pot and bring to a boil. Reduce heat and simmer until beans are desired softness, about 2 to 3 hours.

Place oil in a skillet, crumble in the ground chicken sausage, and sauté until evenly cooked. Add remaining onions and sauté until tender. Stir in green chilies, remaining minced garlic, jalapeño or serrano peppers, and all seasonings. Add sausage mixture to beans along with the cooked chicken. Bring to a boil, then turn to low and simmer for 1 hour.

Serve topped with grated cheese. Garnish with fresh cilantro or chopped scallions. Serve with warm flour or corn tortillas.

JULIE'S CREAMY WHITE CHILI

Creamy white chili from America's dairyland—with just a little kick of heat. Add a cup of corn for a little extra sweetness.

1 tablespoon (15 ml) olive oil
1 pound (453 g) skinless, boneless chicken breast, diced
1 medium white onion, chopped
2 cloves garlic, minced
2-15 oz (850 g) cans Great Northern beans, rinsed and drained
2 cups (472 ml) chicken stock
2-4oz (227 g) cans diced mild green chiles
1 teaspoon (5 g) salt
1 teaspoon (3 g) cumin
1 teaspoon (2.5 g) dried Mexican oregano
½ teaspoon (2.5 g) pepper
½ teaspoon (2 g) cayenne
1 cup (236 ml) sour cream
½ cup (118 ml) whipping cream

Place oil in pan and add chicken, stirring until seared on all sides. Add onions and garlic. Sauté 5 minutes, or until onions are softened. Add beans, chiles, and all seasonings. Bring to a boil, reduce heat, and simmer uncovered for 30 minutes. Remove from heat. Stir in sour cream and whipping cream.

ELEGANT MUSHROOM CHILI

Use portabello caps or any other favorite mushroom in this recipe.

3 tablespoons (45 ml) olive oil
6 cups (450 g) assorted mushrooms, chopped
6 shallots, minced
3 cloves garlic, minced
2 tablespoons (12 g) chili powder
4 cups (950 ml) beef stock
1 cup (250 ml) dry sherry
1-29 ounce (820 g) canned diced tomatoes
2 cups (450 g) canned kidney beans, rinsed and drained
2 cups (280 g) sweet corn

Place oil in a heavy-bottomed pot. Add mushrooms, shallots, and garlic. Cook and stir until liquid evaporates and shallots are softened. Stir in chili powder, beef stock, sherry, beans, and corn. Simmer just 10–20 minutes. Garnish with sour cream and fresh chopped cilantro.

JALAPENO GARDEN GAZPACHO

How can you talk about chile peppers and not add a spicy version of this classic favorite? This gazpacho comes together as I walk through the garden, so no two batches are ever exactly alike. We like ours garnished with chopped avocado and hard-boiled egg.

2 large tomatoes, peeled and chopped
1 green pepper, finely chopped
3 fresh jalapeño peppers, split, seeded, and diced (or other spicy chile)
2 stalks celery, finely chopped
1 cucumber, peeled, seeded, and chopped
1 small onion, finely chopped
2 teaspoons (1.6 g) fresh minced cilantro
1 teaspoon (5 g) fresh chopped chives
1 clove garlic, minced
3 tablespoons (45 g) red wine vinegar
2 tablespoons (30 ml) olive oil
1 teaspoon (5 g) salt
½ teaspoon (2.5 g) Worcestershire sauce
2 cups (475 ml) tomato juice
Black ground pepper

Combine all ingredients in a glass bowl and chill for at least four hours. Serve in small cups, garnished with fresh cilantro or sour cream.

ZACH'S SEVEN BEAN VEGETARIAN CHILI BEANS

Who needs meat when you have this rich, hearty stew of mixed beans and tomatoes?

2 cups (304 g) dry 7-bean blend or any assorted beans
Water
1 medium onion, diced
1 medium red bell pepper, diced
2 cloves garlic, minced
1 cup (236 ml) tomato puree (about 4 Roma tomatoes)
2 quarts (1.9 L) vegetable stock
¼ cup (30 g) Pendery's original chili blend
½ teaspoon (2 g) cayenne
2 teaspoons (10 g) salt
Flour and water paste, if needed

Rinse and sort the beans. Place in large bowl, cover with water, and soak overnight.

Drain and rinse the soaked beans. Place the beans in a crock pot on high setting. Stir in onion, pepper, garlic, tomato puree, chile blend, and cayenne. Add about 2 quarts (1.9 L) stock. Cover and simmer on high for about 4 hours. Taste and adjust seasonings as desired. To thicken, make a paste of 1 tablespoon (7.5 g) flour and 2 tablespoons (30 ml) water. Stir into beans and continue to simmer, with cover removed for the last half hour. Serve with cornbread or over rice.

BLACK BEAN CHILI CON ELOTE

Vegetarian chili featuring fresh corn—the perfect counterpoint to the dark beans and mild chili peppers.

2 tablespoons (30 ml) vegetable oil

1 medium onion

3 cloves garlic

2 fresh Anaheim peppers

2 cups (472 ml) vegetable stock

1 cup (240 ml) tomato puree

2 cups (300 g) corn, cut fresh off cob (about 4 ears)

4 generous cups (720 g) cooked black beans (if you prefer, use 2-15 oz (720 g) cans, rinsed and drained)

2 tablespoons (12 g) Pendery's Fort Worth Light Chile Blend

1 teaspoon (3 g) cumin

1 teaspoon (2.5 g) dried Mexican oregano

1½ teaspoons (7.5 g) salt

½ teaspoon (2.5 g) black pepper

½ teaspoon (1.5 g) cayenne

Chop onion, peppers, and garlic together in a food processor to a coarse puree. Heat oil in heavy-bottomed pot and add vegetables, sautéing until softened. Add stock, tomatoes, and corn. Mash 2 cups (360 g) of the black beans, and stir into the pot along with 2 cups (360 g) of whole beans. Stir in chile blend, cumin, oregano, salt, and peppers. Simmer 30 minutes. Taste, adjust seasonings, and simmer another 30 minutes.

Chili Gone Wild

Where in the world is there a better place to engage in the art of chili making than at a hunting camp, at seaside or in a river cabin? These are the places where many of these recipes came into being—by stalwart chefs celebrating the catch.

Wild chili is born of fresh, local ingredients. Fish and seafood chili has the benefit of being lighter and lower in calories than other types. And wild game is generally leaner and more flavorful than store-bought beef and pork.

We developed a number of our seafood chili recipes while living on the coast of Maine (we only dared to experiment with lobster because of its ready availability). Friends in Florida introduced us to other forms of fish chili and we were inspired by the wild game we tasted in northern Maine and in Montana. We have even gone so far as to pack ground chile into our bags when we head to the Caribbean so that we can make a chili using freshly caught conch.

With a light hand, a mild red or green chile can enhance the natural sweetness of fish and seafood. The gaminess of stronger meats and game birds can be tamped down with a bolder ground chile, perhaps enhanced with a cup of coffee or a bottle of beer.

VENISON CHILI

The guys don't cook much, but this is one recipe they can be relied upon to do well. Camp chili at its best.

4 strips bacon
3 pounds (1.36 kg) ground venison, elk, or buffalo
½ pound (225 g) hot pork sausage
2 large white onions, diced
2 large red bell peppers, diced
6 cups (965 g) diced tomatoes
1 15-oz (450 ml) can tomato sauce
3 ounces (18 g) Pendery's Original chile blend
1 teaspoon (3 g) cumin
1 teaspoon (3 g) Mexican oregano
½ teaspoon (1.5 g) cayenne
1 teaspoon (5 g) black pepper
1 teaspoon (5 g) salt
1 teaspoon (4 g) garlic powder
2 tablespoons (25 g) brown sugar
1-12 ounce (354 ml) bottle beer
2–3 tablespoons (18–27 g) diced jalapeños
2-15 oz (850 g) cans black beans, drained and rinsed

In a large heavy-bottomed pot, fry bacon. Remove from pot and set aside. In the bacon drippings, sauté ground venison and sausage in oil until evenly gray. Add onions and bell peppers and cook until softened. Add tomatoes and tomato sauce, and stir in seasonings, brown sugar, and beer. Add diced jalapeños as desired. Simmer 2–3 hours over low heat. Adjust spices during the last half hour, and add beans. Continue to simmer until beans are heated through.

PHEASANT WHITE CHILI

A delicate chili base for a tender, flavorful bird.

2 tablespoons butter
1 cup green onions, whites and tops, sliced
1 small green or red bell pepper, diced
1 tablespoon (6 g) flour
5 cups (1.2 L) chicken or pheasant stock
4 cups (920 g) pheasant meat, cut into 1″ cubes
1 cup (150 g) fresh corn, cut from cob
2 cups (300 g) cooked white beans
1-4 ounce (115 g) can chopped mild green chilies
2 teaspoons (6 g) ground cumin
1 teaspoon (3 g) Mexican oregano
1 cup (118 ml) half and half
1 tablespoon (15 ml) lime juice

Melt butter in heavy-bottomed pot, and sauté sliced green onions and bell pepper until onions are translucent. Sprinkle flour over vegetables, stirring to incorporate. Add stock and stir until flour is thoroughly blended in. Place pheasant, corn, white beans, and green chiles in pot and simmer gently to heat through. Add half and half, and cook gently for about 10 minutes to incorporate flavors. Finish with a splash of lime juice and serve.

THE KEER GROUP'S PHEASANT RED CHILI

A bold chili from a bold group of intrepid hunters.

3 pounds (1.36 kg) pheasant breasts, thighs, and legs
Salt
Water to cover

2 tablespoons (30 ml) vegetable oil
4 garlic cloves, minced
1 medium onion, finely chopped
2-14.5 ounce (822 g) cans crushed tomato
1-6 ounce (177 ml) can tomato paste
2 cups (472 ml) reserved pheasant stock
3 tablespoons (18 g) chili powder
6 cubes beef bouillon
2 teaspoons (6 g) ground cumin
2 teaspoons (6 g) paprika
2 teaspoons (6 g) oregano
2 teaspoons (10 g) sugar
½ teaspoon (1.5 g) coriander, ground
1 teaspoon (4 g) unsweetened cocoa
2 teaspoons (10 ml) Louisiana hot sauce
1 teaspoon (2.6 g) baking soda
1 teaspoon (2.5 g) cornmeal
1 teaspoon (3 g) flour
1 teaspoon (3.6 ml) water
2-15 ounce (850 g) cans kidney beans, drained and rinsed

CHILI GONE WILD

Cook pheasant pieces in boiling salted water until meat falls off bones. Remove all the meat from the bones and cube. Reserve liquid and set aside.

In a large heavy-bottomed pan, sauté garlic and onion in oil until onions are transparent. Add pheasant, crushed tomatoes, tomato paste, and water and bring to a boil. Add chili powder, bouillon, cumin, paprika, oregano, sugar, coriander, cocoa, hot sauce, and baking soda, stirring to incorporate. Reduce heat to low and simmer for 1 hour. Make a paste of cornmeal, flour, and water and add to the chili, stirring to thicken. Add kidney beans and continue to simmer until beans are heated through, about 15 minutes. Serve with sour cream and chopped scallions.

MAINE HADDOCK CHILI

Any firm-bodied fish can be used in this chili. The addition of Screech Rum from Nova Scotia makes it an authentic North Atlantic dish.

2 pounds (907 g) haddock, cut into 1″ cubes
Vegetable oil
Flour
1 small onion, chopped
1 red bell pepper, chopped
1 cup (161 g) diced tomatoes
2 tablespoons (30 ml) apple cider vinegar
2 cups (304 g) cooked Great Northern beans
2 tablespoons (12 g) mild chile blend
Salt
Pepper
2 tablespoons (30 ml) rum

Dredge cubed fish in flour. Heat 2 tablespoons (30 ml) of oil in a heavy-bottomed pot and sauté the fish until seared on all sides. Remove from pot and set aside.

Add 2 more tablespoons (30 ml) of oil to the pot. Sauté onions and bell peppers until onions are translucent. Stir in tomatoes, vinegar, and beans, and season with chile blend, salt, and pepper. Simmer for a half hour to incorporate all the flavors. In the last 10 minutes, add the haddock back into the pot and finish with a dousing of rum. Cook briefly to warm the fish through. Serve with crusty bread.

MAHI CHILI VERDE

Contributed by some of my favorite Floridians. The Unks family takes advantage of readily available fresh fish, but frozen filets can also be used in this recipe.

2 pounds (907 g) Mahi-Mahi boneless filets
4 fresh sprigs of lemongrass per filet
4 tablespoons (60 ml) grape seed oil
2 medium red onions, chopped
1 medium yellow bell pepper, chopped
4 cloves garlic, minced
2-4 ounce (227 g) cans fire-roasted chiles
2 tablespoons (5 g) fresh basil, chopped
2 tablespoons (5 g) fresh parsley, chopped
2 tablespoons (5 g) fresh cilantro, chopped
1 tablespoon (6 g) chili powder
2 teaspoons (6 g) cayenne pepper
4-19 ounce (2.1 kg) cans cannellini white beans, drained and rinsed
4 cups (950 ml) salsa verde (see recipe in Chapter 7 or use commercial salsa)
1 cup (236 ml) chicken stock
Sea salt and pepper to taste

Fish rub:
2 teaspoons (6 g) paprika
2 teaspoons (6 g) ground cumin
2 teaspoons (6 g) chili powder
2 teaspoons (6 g) cayenne
½ teaspoon (2 g) crushed red pepper
½ teaspoon (2.5 g) ground white pepper
½ teaspoon (2.5 g) sea salt

Rub the fish filets liberally with rub and set aside. Heat grill and lay lemongrass sprigs down, placing one filet over four sprigs. Grill fish about 4–6 minutes on each side. Remove from grill and discard lemongrass sprigs. Flake filets into small pieces and set aside.

Sauté onions, bell pepper, and garlic in grape seed oil until softened. Add the chiles and all seasonings, stirring to incorporate. Add beans and salsa verde. Fold in fish. Simmer on low for one hour, adding chicken stock as needed to achieve desired consistency.

HARPSWELL COVE BLACK BEAN AND LOBSTER CHILI

This recipe, inspired by our dear friends Dick and Patty Ames, is a remarkably delicious and decadent way to serve lobster. Our friend Martha Greenlaw put her own special spin on this recipe in her book Recipes from a Very Small Island.

2 tablespoons (30 ml) vegetable oil
1 medium white onion, chopped
2 cloves garlic, minced
4 cups (605 g) cooked black beans, drained and rinsed
2 cups (472 ml) lobster stock or clam juice
4 cups (605 g) crushed tomatoes
2 fresh jalapeño peppers, diced
2 tablespoons (12 g) chili powder
1 teaspoon (3 g) Mexican oregano
1 teaspoon (3 g) cumin
1 whole bay leaf
4 tablespoons (57 g) butter
2–3 cups (450–680 g) cooked lobster meat, tails cut in 2" pieces, claws whole (about 4
    whole 1½ pound (3 kg) lobsters)
Paprika
2 tablespoons (28 ml) heavy cream

Place oil in a heavy-bottomed pot, and sauté onions and garlic until translucent. Stir in beans, stock, tomatoes, jalapeños, and seasonings. Bring to a boil, then reduce and simmer on low heat for about 2 hours.

Melt butter in a skillet. Add lobster meat and heat gently. Sprinkle a little paprika over lobster and toss to coat, stirring until the lobster is heated through. Just before serving, stir lobster tail pieces into the beans along with the heavy cream. Top with claw meat and serve.

WHITE SHRIMP CHILI

This flavorful tomato-free base is a nice backdrop for fresh seafood. Try lobster in place of the shrimp for an elegant dish.

2 tablespoons (30 ml) vegetable oil
1 medium white onion, chopped
3 stalks celery, chopped
1 large red bell pepper, chopped
2 tablespoon (20 g) chopped chipotle chiles in adobo
2 teaspoons (6 g) ground roasted cumin
2 teaspoons (6 g) dried Mexican oregano
1-12 ounce (354 ml) bottle beer
3 cups chicken (720 ml) or seafood stock
2-15 ounce (650 g) cans white beans, rinsed and drained
1 pound large shrimp, peeled and deveined
½ cup (20 g) cilantro, finely chopped
Juice of 1 lime

Place oil in heavy-bottomed pot and sauté onions, celery, peppers until softened. Add chiles, cumin, and oregano, and stir in beer, stock, and white beans. Simmer for 20 minutes. Just before serving, stir in raw shrimp and simmer about 5 minutes, or until shrimp are translucent. Add cilantro and lime juice to the pot, and serve immediately.

SAUSAGE AND SEAFOOD CHILI

Make your sausage chili base ahead of time, and add your choice of seafood just before serving.

3 tablespoons (45 ml) vegetable oil
1 pound (453 g) hot Italian sausage
2 large onions, chopped
1 large celery stalk, chopped
2 red bell peppers, chopped
4 cloves garlic, blanched and minced
4 cups (640 g) crushed tomatoes
2 teaspoons (6 g) Mexican oregano
2 cups 472 ml) seafood stock
2 cups (472 ml) dry red wine
½ cup (125 ml) mild red chili paste
2 teaspoons (6 g) ground roast cumin
1 tablespoon (5 g) salt
12 littleneck clams
12 mussels, scrubbed and de-bearded
12 large shrimp, peeled and deveined
¾ pound (340 g) bay scallops

Heat oil in heavy-bottomed pot. Place sausages in oil and brown on all sides. And onion, celery, garlic, and bell peppers and sauté until tender. Add tomatoes, oregano, seafood stock, wine, chili paste, cumin, salt, and cayenne. Bring to a boil, and then reduce heat and simmer for about 1 hour. Remove sausages from chili, cut into bite-size pieces, and return to pot.

Just before serving, bring chili base to a boil. Add clams and mussels. Cover and cook until shellfish open. (Discard any that do not open.) Stir in shrimp and scallops and cook just until translucent, about 5 minutes. Serve immediately.

CHILI-STYLE MUSSELS

Delicious mussels with the spice of chorizo and chiles, softened and finished into a rich sauce with the addition of cream.

4 ounces (115 g) chorizo sausage, casing removed and chopped
2 tablespoons (30 ml) olive oil
1 small white onion, finely chopped
1 serrano or other small hot chile, split, seeded and minced
3 garlic cloves, minced
½ cup (80 g) diced tomato, about 2 Roma tomatoes
1 teaspoon (3 g) Mexican oregano
½ bottle (180 ml) Corona beer
2 pounds (907 g) fresh mussels, scrubbed and de-bearded
¼ cup (42 ml) heavy cream
Fresh cilantro, chopped

In a large sauté pan, cook the chorizo until crumbled and cooked through. Add onion, garlic, and chile. Cook just until softened. Stir in tomatoes and oregano, and continue to cook for about 2 minutes. Add beer and bring to a boil. Add mussels, cover, and cook until shells have opened, 5–7 minutes. Remove mussels from sauce and set aside in large serving bowl. Discard any that do not open.

Stir in cream, and cook over medium heat for 3 minutes. Pour sauce over mussels. Garnish with chopped cilantro and serve.

WILD BOAR AND PUMPKIN CHILI

Leaner and darker than regular pork, the flavor of wild boar is enhanced by the sweetness of the pumpkin and dark beer.

2 tablespoons (30 ml) vegetable oil
1 large onion, chopped
1 large red bell pepper, chopped
2 cloves garlic, minced
3 pounds (1.36 kg) wild boar, coarsely ground
1-10 ounce (295 ml) can pumpkin puree
1 cup (160 g) crushed tomatoes
1-6 ounce (180 ml) can tomato paste
1 cup (240 ml) dark beer
1 cup (236 ml) chicken stock
3 tablespoons (18 g) ancho chili powder
2 teaspoons (6 g) roasted ground cumin
1 teaspoon (3 g) cinnamon
1 teaspoon (5 g) salt
2 cups (320 g) cooked black beans, rinsed and drained

In a heavy-bottomed pot, sauté onion, bell pepper, and garlic in oil until vegetables are softened. Stir in ground meat, breaking up until crumbled and cooked evenly. Add pumpkin, tomatoes, paste, beer, stock, and seasonings. Bring to a boil, then reduce heat and simmer uncovered for about two hours, adding more stock as needed. Adjust seasonings and add beans. Continue to simmer until beans are heated through.

Chile Sauces, Salsas, and Rubs

For many cooks, the art of the salsa is almost as important as that of the chili. I have started to see competitive salsa competitions alongside chili events, giving chefs the chance to celebrate the fresh chile pepper in all its glory. Salsas come in raw and cooked version, as well as in varieties of red and green. Fruit often makes an appearance, as do tomatoes, tomatillos, beans and onions.

To me, the best way to come up with a salsa recipe is to walk through the garden, grabbing a bit of this and a bit of that to make something fresh and unique. My salsas are rarely the same twice in a row, and that's the way I like it. A little fresh mint or the crunch of a fresh carrot creates a fun surprise, as does grated zucchini or yellow squash. My husband likes chunky salsa and I prefer it a little smoother, so whether I cook a batch or make a salsa fresca, I often keep about half of it in the food processor for a few extra pulses. Fresh salsa is best the day it is made, so any leftovers usually go into a cooked sauce or pot of chili.

A good rule of thumb is to use one hot pepper for every three tomatoes. If you like it milder, use a chile low on the Scoville scale and make sure to remove seeds and veins. If you prefer it hotter, choose a chile on the higher end of the scale. Add tomatillos, garlic, cilantro and onions as desired. Sautéed onion provides a sweeter, caramelized flavor and a roasted chile will add a little smokiness. A squeeze of lime or lemon will brighten the flavors and help to quiet the heat.

BASIC RED CHILE SAUCE

A good basic sauce for enchiladas and burritos or a base for your chili pot. Combine using a variety of dried chiles to achieve the flavor and heat you desire.

8 reconstituted New Mexico chiles, drained (See page 11 for instructions on how to reconstitute dried chiles.)
2 cloves garlic
1 cup (236 ml) beef stock
1 teaspoon (3 g) cumin
½ teaspoon (1.5 g) Mexican oregano
½ teaspoon (2.5 g) salt
1 teaspoon (5 ml) olive oil
1 tablespoon (7.5 g) sugar
1 tablespoon (15 ml) tomato paste

Place softened chiles, garlic, stock, and seasonings in a food processor and puree until smooth. Strain sauce through a sieve to give it a smooth consistency.

Place oil in a saucepan and pour in strained chiles. Add sugar and tomato paste and simmer on low for 10 minutes. Taste and adjust salt. Makes about 1 cup of thick red sauce. Add stock to thin it for use in enchiladas or burritos.

GREEN CHILE SAUCE

We make large batches of this sauce and freeze in one-cup servings. Use as a base for your white and green chili recipes.

12 Anaheim chiles, roasted, peeled, seeded, chopped
1 onion, chopped
1 clove garlic, minced
½ teaspoon (2.5 g) salt
1 cup (236 ml) chicken broth

Place chiles, onion, garlic, and salt in a skillet with broth. Bring to a boil, and then reduce heat. Simmer for 15 minutes. Take off heat and let cool. Puree in a food processer.

FRESH GARDEN SALSA

Best served the day you make it. Fresh tomatoes don't really care for refrigeration so take any leftover salsa, blend it until smooth, cook for a few minutes, and store for use on enchiladas or tacos.

1 clove garlic, peeled
1 Anaheim green chile, seeded and cut into chunks
1 small red onion, quartered
2 fresh jalapeños, seeded
3 large tomatoes, chopped
3 tablespoons (7.5 g) fresh cilantro
½ teaspoon (2.5 g) salt
Juice from ½ lime

Place garlic, chile, red onion, and jalapeños in food processor until evenly chopped. Place in bowl. Hand chop tomatoes and add to bowl. Stir in fresh cilantro and salt, and squeeze in lime juice. Cover and let sit at room temperature for 30 minutes before serving.

FRESH SALSA VERDE

Tomatillos are fairly easy to grow, so if you have a garden, add them to your mix. This salsa is positively addictive. Make it as mild or as hot as you like. And make plenty—it's great with tortilla chips or served over enchiladas.

1 pound (454 g) tomatillos, husks removed and cut into quarters
1 small white onion
3 cloves garlic, peeled
1 Poblano chile, seeded and cut into chunks
2 jalapeños, seeds removed
½ cup (20 g) fresh cilantro
Juice of ½ lime
1 teaspoon (5 g) salt

In a food processor, combine all ingredients. Use the pulse setting to coarsely chop, stopping to scrape the bowl as needed. Cover and let sit at room temperature for 30 minutes before serving.

MANGO BLACK BEAN SALSA

Perfectly fresh mangos, preferably right off the tree, are the magic ingredient in this recipe. Ripe peaches make a great substitute.

1 large mango, chopped
⅓ cup (51 g) red onion, chopped
1-15 ounce (425 g) can black beans, drained and rinsed
¼ cup (10 g) freshly chopped cilantro
1 jalapeño pepper, seeded and minced
Juice of 1 lime

Combine mango, red onion, black beans, cilantro, and jalapeño in a medium bowl. Squeeze lime juice over mixture. Stir well, cover, and refrigerate until ready to serve.

RANCH SAUCE

We use this basic sauce on grilled steaks, over fried eggs, even with thick slices of fried polenta.

1 clove garlic, peeled
2 fresh jalapeños, split and seeded
1 small white onion, quartered
1 fresh Poblano chile, seeded and cut into chunks
2 tablespoons (30 ml) olive oil
4 Roma tomatoes, chopped
¼ teaspoon (1 g) salt

Chop garlic, jalapeños, onion, and chile in food processor, pulsing until everything is coarsely chopped. Place oil in a skillet and add the chopped vegetables, sautéing until softened. Add chopped tomatoes and simmer over low heat just until cooked.

CARIBBEAN HOT SAUCE

Sweet and spicy, with a big kick. Modify the chiles as desired to get the heat you want.

12 habanero chiles, split and seeded
2 ripe mangos, peeled and cut into chunks
1 cup (260 ml) yellow prepared mustard
¼ cup (47 g) brown sugar, packed
¼ cup (60 ml) apple cider vinegar
1 tablespoon (5 g) curry powder
1 tablespoon (6 g) roasted ground cumin
1 tablespoon (6 g) chili powder
½ teaspoon (2.5 g) salt

Wear rubber gloves to split and seed your habaneros. Puree habaneros and mango together in food processor. (Make sure to avert face from the processor tube—habanero fumes are hard on the eyes and nose!) Add the rest of the ingredients and process until smooth. Refrigerate in glass container.

LUTHER'S HABANERO SAUCE

Muy picante! A glorious sauce that we use to add a sweet zing to any recipe. Luther uses fresh pineapple and organic carrots to give the base its pleasing sweetness.

1 pound habanero chiles, split and seeded

1 medium white onion, peeled and cut into chunks

4 cups (946 ml) apple cider vinegar

3 pounds (1.36 kg) organic carrots, peeled and cut into chunks

2 pounds (907 g) fresh pineapple, cored and cut into chunks

Place all ingredients in a large stock pot. Bring to a boil, and then turn heat to low and simmer until carrots are soft enough to puree. Working in batches, transfer cooked mixture to a food processor and puree until smooth. Store in refrigerator.

CHILE CHEESE SAUCE

A southwestern twist on classic white sauce; add a swirl over chili or to use as a topping over cornbread casserole.

1 small onion, quartered

2 cloves garlic, peeled

1 red bell pepper, quartered

2 jalapeño peppers, split and seeds removed

2 tablespoons (30 ml) olive oil

1 teaspoon (3 g) cumin

1 teaspoon (4 g) ancho chili powder

½ teaspoon (2.5 g) salt

2 tablespoons (12 g) flour

1 cup (236 ml) chicken stock

1 cup (120 g) Monterey Jack cheese, shredded

Place onion, garlic, bell pepper, and jalapeños in food processor and pulse until very finely chopped. Place oil in saucepan and add processed vegetables, sautéing until tender. Sprinkle seasonings and flour over vegetables. Cook, stirring constantly for about 2 minutes, or until fully incorporated. Stir in chicken stock and simmer for about 10 minutes, until sauce has thickened. Add cheese and stir until melted and blended into the sauce.

QUESO BLANCO DIP

Classic Southwestern white cheese dip, turned up a notch with hot green chiles.

1 cup (120 g) Monterey Jack cheese, shredded

1-4 ounce (113 g) can hot, diced green chiles (use mild green chiles, if you prefer)

¼ cup (120 ml) light cream

2 tablespoon (38 g) onions, chopped fine

1 teaspoon (3 g) ground cumin

½ teaspoon (2.5 g) salt

Put all ingredients in a small crock pot on low setting. Cook, stirring occasionally, until cheese is melted and ingredients are nicely blended. Serve with tortilla chips.

CLASSIC CHILI DIP

This quick classic recipe from Velveeta is a staple on game day.

2 cups (300 g) leftover chili without beans

16 ounces (240 g) Velveeta cheese, cut into chunks

Microwave chili and Velveeta in a microwavable bowl for about 5 minutes, pausing halfway to stir melted cheese into chili. Transfer dip into a small crock pot and heat on low. Serve with chunks of French bread or tortilla chips.

COWBOY STEAK RUB

Traditional cowboy seasonings make beef sing with flavor. Rub onto both sides of beef steaks and grill until medium rare. Serve with a side of rice and red chile sauce.

1 teaspoon (4 g) ground ancho chile

1 teaspoon (4 g) fine ground espresso coffee

1 teaspoon (4 g) brown sugar

½ teaspoon (1.5 g) dry mustard

½ teaspoon (1.5 g) roasted ground cumin

½ teaspoon (2.5 g) salt

In a large bowl, combine ground chile, coffee, brown sugar, mustard, cumin, and salt to make a rub.

HOT PEPPER VINEGAR

My kitchen can't be without this basic necessity—we use it for marinating chicken, sprinkling on rice dishes, and serving with collard greens. A bottle of it is always a part of my pantry.

Fresh jalapeño peppers

White vinegar

Wash peppers and slice them in half, removing the seeds. Finely dice them and pack into a jar. Bring vinegar to a boil and pour over peppers, making sure peppers are completely covered. Add lid or cork to bottle and store in refrigerator for a couple of weeks before using.

CHIPOTLE PEANUT DRESSING

This tangy dressing is good on everything from a wedge of iceberg to grilled chicken skewers.

¼ cup (60 ml) rice wine vinegar
2 tablespoons (22 g) smooth peanut butter
2 teaspoons (10 ml) chipotle paste
1 tablespoon (7 g) chopped fresh ginger
1 tablespoon (15 ml) soy sauce
1 tablespoon (21 g) honey
½ cup vegetable oil
½ teaspoon (2.5 g) salt

Whisk together all ingredients.

Chili Leftovers

My family is generally not a big fan of leftovers. The one exception to this rule is chili. In fact, chili just keeps getting better as it rests, the flavors continuing to meld and develop over a couple of days. It is a sad day when we look in the refrigerator and realize the last of the chili has disappeared.

Most of our "leftover" chili gets eaten by the bowlful, but I do have a couple of special dishes that call for their own batch of chili, or at least an extra-big batch that can be used later in the week for a casserole. For potlucks or family get-togethers, sometimes a casserole is the best way to serve your chili, and I relish the opportunity to top a batch with a moist crust of cornbread or tamale dough.

Mashed potatoes with chili is a surprisingly comforting meal, and I have friends who can't bear to eat their chili leftovers without a base of pasta noodles. I grew up with chili and rice, so while my "first day" meal is probably a straight bowl of red, often the next day sees my chili sidling up to a nice scoop of rice and refried beans.

FRITO PIE

The simplest of chili casseroles—and the most popular with kids. Variations are as many as there are types of chili. The classic burger-and-beans type is traditional, but try it with chunky Texas chili for a gourmet treat. Sauté onions first to mellow the onion flavor.

1 tablespoon (15 ml) vegetable oil
1 large onion, chopped
3 cups (130 g) Fritos original corn chips
2 cups (225 g) your favorite chili, heated
1 cup (112 g) grated Monterey cheese
Sour cream, chopped black olives and green onions

Preheat oven to 350 degrees. Sauté onions until caramelized. Set aside. Place 2 cups of Fritos in baking dish. Arrange onions and half of grated cheese over Fritos. Cover with heated chili. Top with remaining corn chips and grated cheese. Bake at 350 degrees for 30 minutes. Garnish with a dollop of sour cream, black olives, and chopped green onions.

SOUTHWESTERN SHEPHERD'S PIE

3 cups (700 g) leftover chili
1 cup (120 g) shredded cheddar cheese
1 cup (180 g) fresh or frozen corn
2 cups (425 g) prepared mashed potatoes

Place leftover chili in an ovenproof casserole dish. Layer cheese and then corn on top. Top the entire surface of the casserole with mashed potatoes. Add a pat of butter on top. Bake 30 minutes in a 350 degree oven.

CHILI SPOON BREAD CASSEROLE

I love this cozy casserole—just as good with plain vegetarian chili beans as it is with hearty beef chili.

3 cups (420 ml) leftover chili
1 cup (220 g) fresh or frozen corn kernels

Cornbread:
½ cup (50 g) white flour
1 cup (170 g) yellow stone-ground cornmeal
2 teaspoons (10 ml) molasses
2 teaspoons (7.5 g) baking powder
½ teaspoon (2.5 g) salt
2 eggs
1 cup (240 ml) milk
1 small onion, grated
2 fresh jalapeños, split, seeded, and diced
¼ cup (60 ml) vegetable oil
1 cup (120 g) sharp cheddar cheese, grated

Preheat oven to 375 degrees. Place 3 cups (420 ml) of chili in a lightly greased 3-quart casserole. Spread corn evenly over chili. Make cornbread by combining all ingredients in a bowl, stirring until batter is smooth. Pour over top of chili. Bake at 375 degrees for about 40 minutes or until cornbread is golden brown.

TAMALE PIE

Use real tamale dough to give this chili pie an authentic Tex-Mex flavor. I like to use the sweet and fragrant Chili with Apples and Raisins as my filling.

3 cups leftover chili

Tamale dough:
1 ½ cups (190 g) masa harina
6 tablespoons (86 g) butter
½ teaspoon (2 g) baking powder
¼ teaspoon (1.25 g) salt
¼ cup (60 ml) cream
¾ cup (177 ml) chicken stock
½ cup (56 g) Monterey Jack cheese, grated

Preheat oven to 375 degrees. Combine masa harina, butter, baking powder, salt, and cream in a food processor. Pulse to incorporate butter and create a uniform dough. With the processor running, add chicken stock a little at a time until dough has a moist, soft consistency that will spread easily into the pan.

Spread half the dough into a lightly oiled 13" x 9" baking dish. Spoon chili over bottom crust. Top with remaining cornmeal dough. Bake at 375 degrees for 45 minutes. During the last 10 minutes of cooking, add the shredded cheese to the top crust and bake until cheese is melted.

Serve immediately out of the oven with a gravy boat of red chile sauce for topping.

GREEN CHICKEN CHILE CHILAQUILES

Chilaquiles are the perfect recipe to use up leftovers. Start with stale tortillas and add any filling you prefer. This one uses green chile sauce and pre-cooked chicken, but any leftover chili would do.

3 tablespoons (45 ml) vegetable oil
12 stale corn tortillas, each cut into 6 wedges
3 cups (700 g) cooked shredded chicken
3 cups (480 g) salsa verde (recipe in Chapter 7)
¾ cup (225 ml) sour cream
2 cups (222 g) Monterey jack cheese, grated

Heat vegetable oil in large skillet and fry tortilla wedges until they are softened and chewy. Remove from oil and drain on paper towels.

In a large mixing bowl, combine chicken, 2½ cups (400 g) salsa verde, and sour cream.

Preheat the oven to 350 degrees. Lightly oil a 4-quart casserole dish. Spoon in about ½ cup (118 ml) of salsa, enough to coat the bottom of the dish. Place about one third of the tortilla wedges in the casserole, and top with half of the chicken mixture. Spread about 1 cup (120 g) of cheese over the chicken. Repeat the layers, ending with a layer of tortilla wedges on top. Cover with foil. Bake 30 minutes. Garnish with an extra dollop of sour cream and chopped ripe olives.

CHILI-MAC

Classic comfort food. Make mild or spicy to suit the age and inclination of your guests.

1 cup (45 g) dry elbow macaroni

4 cups (920 g) ground beef chili with beans

2 cups (240 g) Monterey Jack cheese, grated

Cook elbow macaroni according to package directions. Place drained macaroni in a bowl and stir in chili. Transfer mixture to a greased 13" x 9" baking dish. Cover with foil and bake at 375 degrees for 30 minutes. Remove foil and cover with grated cheese. Bake for 10 minutes or until cheese is melted and bubbly.

CHILI ENCHILADAS

I often make my Texas chili with large chunks of beef—the leftovers are perfect for making these flavorful enchiladas.

4 cups (605 g) thick Texas beef chili without beans
1 small onion, chopped
1 8 ounce (225 g) block cream cheese
1 cup (240 ml) enchilada sauce
12 corn tortillas
2 cups (240 g) cheddar cheese, grated

Place chili in a saucepan and warm through, reducing sauce if necessary to create a thick stew. Fold in onions and cream cheese.

Warm enchilada sauce in a small skillet. Dip tortillas into sauce one at a time, turning to warm and soften on both sides. Fill each tortilla with a large spoonful of the chili mixture and top with a large sprinkle of cheddar cheese. Roll up tortillas and place seam side down side by side in a greased 13" x 9" baking dish. Cover tortillas with enchilada sauce and remaining cheese. Bake in a preheated 375 degree oven until hot and bubbly, about 20 minutes. Serve piping hot with sour cream and chopped jalapeños to garnish.

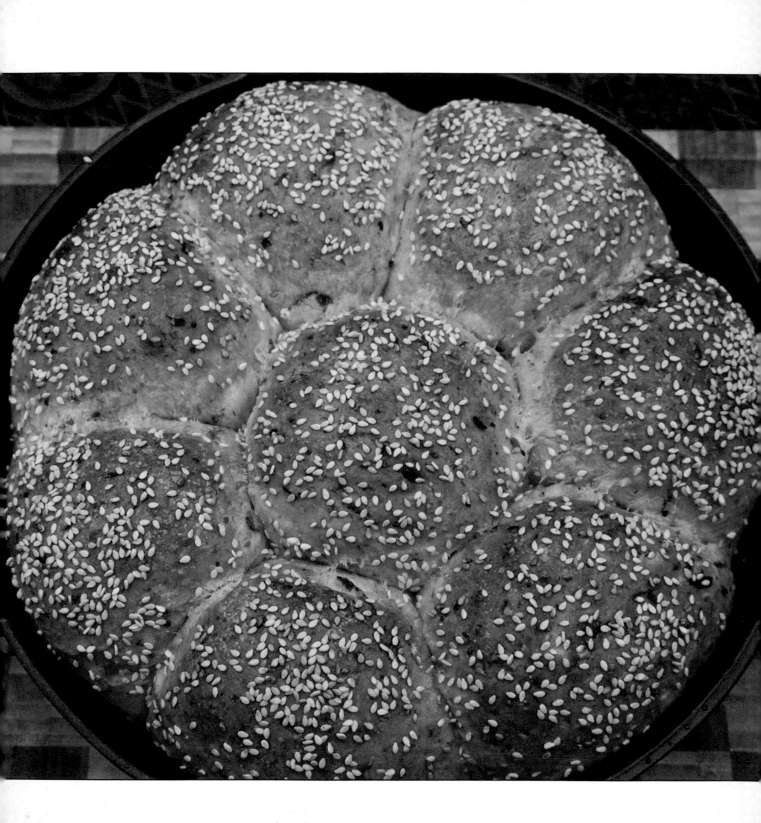

Breads, Tortillas, and Side Dishes

As much as we hate to admit it, even we cannot live on chili alone. Moist cornbread, tender tortillas, homemade chips—this chapter contains some of our favorite accompaniments to a bowl of red.

We tend to make big batches of tortillas so they are available whenever the mood strikes. Keep your freshly made tortillas in a tightly sealed bag at room temperature. Never refrigerate them—the cold draws moisture out of the bread and causes them to go stale three times faster. If you want to store tortillas for later use, the best way is in the freezer. Tortillas can be kept there for up to three months.

We place tortillas in the freezer in batches that we can use in one meal. Place them in a plastic bag and then wrap in foil to prevent freezer burn. When you are ready to use them, let them defrost naturally at room temperature. When thawed, remove them from the plastic, wrap them in foil and place in a 350 degree oven for 5 to 10 minutes. They will taste almost as good as new. Use these as soon as possible though. Once cooled, they will be drier than the originals.

ZUCCHINI CROWN ROLLS

Gorgeous, moist rolls that pair well with spicy chili.

2 cups (300 g) zucchini, grated
Salt
5 cups (500 g) flour
1 package yeast
¼ cup freshly (45 g) grated Parmesan cheese
1 teaspoon (5 g) salt
1 teaspoon (5 g) black pepper
2 tablespoons (30 ml) olive oil
About 2 cups (475 ml) lukewarm water
Milk and sesame seeds for glaze

Grate zucchini and sprinkle lightly with salt. Place in a colander to drain for about 30 minutes. Squeeze thoroughly and pat dry to remove excess moisture.

Mix the flour, yeast, Parmesan, salt, and black pepper together. Mix in the oil and zucchini. Stir in 1 cup water, and then add remaining water a little at a time, stirring until your dough is firm. Turn dough out of bowl and knead lightly, dusting with flour as needed. Place ball of dough in an oiled mixing bowl, turning it once to oil the top of dough. Cover with a towel and set in a sunny place to rise. Dough should double in size. Time for rising will vary. On a warm, sunny day, less than an hour should do it.

Punch down dough and knead it lightly. Cut into 8 equal pieces, rolling each into a ball. Place balls into a lightly oiled 12″ baking dish. Brush the tops with milk and sprinkle with sesame seeds. Cover with towel and let rise about 30 minutes.

TOBY'S TEX MEX CORNBREAD

My friend Toby shared this recipe years ago, and it remains one of our favorites. Moist and packed with flavor, it's almost a meal in itself.

1½ cups (255 g) cornmeal
1 cup (236 ml) milk
¾ teaspoon (3.75 g) salt
½ cup (115 g) melted butter
½ teaspoon (2 g) baking soda
1 (14- ounce) (420 ml) can cream-style corn
½ pound (225 g) Monterey Jack cheese, grated
6 green onions, whites and greens diced
1 (4-ounce) (120 ml) can diced green chiles

Mix cornmeal, milk, salt, butter, soda, and canned corn together. Pour half the batter into a 10" (25.4 cm) Dutch oven. Layer the cheese, onions, and green chiles over the batter. Pour the rest of the batter on top. Bake at 350 degrees for 35–40 minutes.

FLOUR TORTILLAS

Softer and more pliable than corn tortillas, these flour tortillas are best served hot off the griddle. If you can't serve immediately, hold wrapped in foil until ready to serve.

1 cup (99 g) white flour
½ teaspoon (2 g) baking powder
½ teaspoon (2.5 g) salt
2–3 tablespoons (30–45 g) lard
4–6 tablespoons (60–90 ml) water

Place all ingredients except the water in a food processor and blend until dough is a soft crumble. Add 4 tablespoons water and process for another minute, until dough begins to form a ball. Add 1 tablespoon of water and blend until dough is soft but not sticky. If the dough is still too dry, add 1 more tablespoon and process for another 30 seconds.

Form dough into a ball and wrap in plastic wrap. Set aside for a half hour. When you are ready to cook tortillas, divide the dough into 6 pieces and roll each into a ball. (Keep dough you are not working with under a towel.)

Take the first ball and dredge in flour. Press out into a 3″ circle on a floured surface. Use a rolling pin to roll the dough into a 6″ circle, rolling and turning a quarter turn until dough reaches the size you want. You can roll dough up to 7 or 8″ in diameter. Just be aware, the thinner they are, the more delicate they will be. Set finished tortilla aside under a towel as you complete the rest.

Heat dry skillet to medium heat. Cook tortilla about one minute on each side, or until the tortilla is dry and spotted brown on both sides. Remove the cooked tortillas from the heat and hold on a plate with a large pot lid over them to continue steaming. When the stack is done, serve immediately. (If reheating is required, wrap in foil and heat in a 300 degree oven for a few minutes.)

FRIED TORTILLA CHIPS

1 package yellow corn tortillas or white flour tortillas
Vegetable oil for frying
Salt

Cut each tortilla into six evenly sized wedges.

Heat oil on medium-high heat in a heavy skillet or Dutch oven. (I like to use cast iron for frying.) Your oil is ready when one test tortilla bubbles and floats within a couple of seconds. Add chips in small batches of 8 to 10 at a time, turning once so that chips are evenly cooked on both sides. Go for a golden color; chips that are actually browned are overcooked. Remove each chip as soon as it is done. Drain on stack of paper towels. Season with salt while chips are still warm.

MEXICAN RICE

A side of rice can help take down the heat of a hot chili, even this one that carries just a bite of jalapeño. If you like it spicier, add a shake of cayenne to the seasonings.

2 tablespoons (30 g) butter
1 medium onion, chopped
1 red bell pepper, seeded and diced
1 clove garlic, minced
1 cup (180 g) white rice
2 cups (472 ml) chicken stock
1 large tomato, seeded and chopped
1 jalapeño, seeded and diced
2 teaspoons (6 g) chili powder
1 teaspoon (3 g) roasted ground cumin

Place butter in a heavy-bottomed saucepan. Sauté onions, bell pepper, and garlic, cooking until softened. Add the rice, stirring until lightly golden. Add stock, tomato, jalapeño, chili powder, and cumin. Cover and simmer for 5 minutes.

Pour rice mixture into a buttered one-quart casserole. Bake at 375 degrees or until the stock is fully absorbed, about 40 minutes.

REFRIED BEANS

Refried beans are a staple of the Southwest and especially good sidled up next to a ladle of red chili. If you wish, sauté onions and garlic before mashing your beans, and add chili powder, salt, or other seasonings after frying.

4 cups (605 g) cooked beans
4 tablespoons (60 ml) lard or vegetable oil
Salt

Place oil or lard in large heavy-bottomed skillet and heat it gently. Add a ladle full of whole beans and start mashing them into the oil. When those are mashed, add another ladle full, continuing the process until all the beans have been mashed and lightly fried. Add a little stock or bean liquid to get the consistency you prefer. Season or salt as desired.

GERTIE'S FRIED CORN

An old southern recipe that pairs beautifully with chili dishes.

3 tablespoons (45 ml) bacon drippings
10 ears of sweet corn, cut fresh off cob
1 red bell pepper, diced
1 small onion, diced
1 teaspoon (3 g) white flour
½ cup (120 ml) cream
2 tablespoons (4 g) fresh chopped parsley
Salt and pepper to taste

Heat bacon drippings in a large skillet just until sizzling. Add corn, bell pepper, and onions, and sauté until corn begins to brown. Sprinkle flour over corn and stir to incorporate. Stir in cream. Salt and pepper to taste.

Libations and Desserts

No celebration of chili and chile peppers would be complete without the sweets and the drinks that incorporate and accompany them.

Chili is remarkably adept at playing well with other flavors. Chile and chocolate are actually a magical pairing, the one adding a bite of mystery and spice, the other a smooth, mellowing effect. Cinnamon, fruit, caramel and salt are also wonderful combinations with chile. The gentle flavor of creamy ice cream, cream cheese and sour cream provide a soothing counterpoint to intense spice.

When it comes to drinks, there is no end to the rums and tequila offerings available, combined with lime, sugar and salt to transport you on a temporary vacation to the Caribbean. Citrus flavors can be a welcome relief alongside a hot bowl of red, playing naturally on the taste buds to tamp down the spiciness of the chiles.

Of course, beer was seemingly made with chili in mind, and you can make a game of matching the right chili flavors to the right beer. For wine lovers, there are actually good pairings too. See the suggested beer and wine pairings at the end of this chapter.

As a child, my drink of choice with chili was milk. I think I knew instinctively that this was the best way to chase away the heat. These days, I like to end my meal with the whimsical combination of ice cream and beer in the Guinness Stout Float.

No celebration of chili and chile peppers would be without the sweets and the drinks that incorporate and accompany them.

Chili is remarkably adept at playing well with other flavors. Chile and chocolate are actually a magical pairing, the one adding a bite of mystery and spice, the other a smooth, mellowing effect. Cinnamon, fruit, caramel and salt are also wonderful combinations with chile. The gentle flavor of creamy ice cream, cream cheese and sour cream provide a soothing counterpoint to intense spice.

When it comes to drinks, there is no end to the rums and tequila offerings available, combined with lime, sugar and salt to transport you on a temporary vacation to the Caribbean. Citrus flavors can be a welcome relief alongside a hot bowl of red, playing naturally on the taste buds to tamp down the spiciness of the chiles.

Of course, beer was seemingly made with chili in mind, and you can make a game of matching the right chili flavors to the right beer. For wine lovers, there are actually good pairings too. See the suggested beer and wine pairings at the end of this chapter.

As a child, my drink of choice with chili was milk. I think I knew instinctively that this was the best way to chase away the heat. These days, I like to end my meal with the whimsical combination of ice cream and beer in the Guinness Stout Float.

LIBATIONS

CISSIE'S KICKASS MARGARITA

No, really.

2 ounces (59 ml) tequila
½ ounce (15 ml) orange liqueur
2 ounces (59 ml) lime juice

Place all ingredients into a shaker with ice. Shake and strain into salt-rimmed margarita glass.

PINEAPPLE HABANERO COCKTAIL

A perfect use of our homemade habanero sauce—and a tangy start to cocktail hour! Be gentle when adding the habanero sauce. It's easy to add a little extra afterward for those adventurous enough for a bigger kick.

1½ ounces (45 ml) tequila
¾ ounce (22 ml) orange liqueur
¾ ounce (22 ml) fresh lime juice
2 ounces (59 ml) pineapple juice
2 drops of Luther's Habanero sauce (see Chapter 7)

Shake all ingredients together with ice. Strain into tall glass filled with ice. Garnish with pineapple.

JAMAICAN STOUT PUNCH

Of course, the true Jamaican recipe calls for one whole raw egg. Either way, the recipe is famous for its ability to put that "get up and go" back in your stride. A sprinkle of cayenne adds a bit of kick.

2 cups (472 ml) Guinness stout
½-3 ounce (88 ml) can sweetened condensed milk
½ teaspoon (2 g) nutmeg
1 teaspoon (4 g) cinnamon
¼ cup (60 ml) Egg Beaters
¼ teaspoon (2 g) cayenne

Place all ingredients in a blender and blend until smooth. Transfer to a covered pitcher and chill thoroughly before serving.

FROZEN WATERMELON MARGARITA

Wonderful and refreshing, especially alongside hot chiles and chips.

1 cup (236 ml) tequila
½ cup (118 ml) triple sec
½ cup (118 ml) melon liqueur
1 cup (236 ml) sour mix
4 cups (900 ml) cubed, seeded watermelon
1 fresh jalapeño pepper, seeded and chopped
4 cups (900 ml) ice

Blend all ingredients together, adding ice one cup at a time to fully crush it. Serve in a pitcher with wedges of fresh watermelon.

HABANERO CUBANA

Our twist on the classic south-of-the-border hangover remedy. A bowl of chili on the side? Absolutely!

1 ounce (30 ml) fresh lime juice
3 drops Tabasco sauce
3 dashes soy sauce
2 dashes Worcestershire sauce
2 drops Luther's habanero sauce
Fresh ground pepper
1-12 ounce (360 ml) bottle of beer

Rim a pint glass with a lime slice and coarse salt. Place the fresh lime juice and all the sauces into a large chilled pint glass. Pour beer into glass, being careful not to touch the salt. Serve.

DESSERTS

CHOCOLATE CHILE PEPPER CUPCAKES

A mildly surprising bite in an otherwise conventional chocolate cupcake—even the cream cheese frosting carries through on the ancho flavor.

3 tablespoons (43 g) butter, softened
1½ cups (287 g) sugar
2 eggs
¾ teaspoon (3.4 ml) rum extract
1 cup (133 g) all-purpose flour
¼ teaspoon (1 g) baking soda
2 teaspoons (7.5 g) baking powder
¾ cup (68 g) unsweetened cocoa powder
1½ teaspoons (3 g) ancho chili powder
⅛ teaspoon (.5 g) salt
1 cup (236 ml) milk

ANCHO CREAM CHEESE FROSTING

1 teaspoon (2 g) ancho chili powder
½ teaspoon (1 g) cinnamon
4 cups (520 g) powdered sugar
8 ounces (130 g) cream cheese, softened
½ cup (115 g) butter, softened
½ teaspoon (2.5 ml) rum extract

In a large mixing bowl, cream butter and sugar until fluffy. Beat in eggs and rum extract. Add flour, soda, powder, cocoa, chili powder, and salt. Mix slowly as you add milk. Scrape sides, and then beat well until batter is smooth and glossy.

Line cupcake tins with papers and fill about ⅔ full. Bake at 350 degrees for about 15–17 minutes, or until center doesn't leave impression when touched.

For frosting, stir chili powder and cinnamon with the confectioners' sugar. Beat cream cheese, butter, and rum extract into sugar until frosting is smooth.

Cool cupcakes and top with frosting.

AVOCADO-JALAPEÑO ICE CREAM

Smooth, creamy, and delicious—the perfect after-dinner antidote to a meal of spicy chili. The jalapeño provides only a tickle to the taste buds.

2 cups (475 ml) of ripe avocado
1 tablespoon (15 ml) lime juice
1 fresh jalapeño pepper, stemmed, seeded, and diced
¾ cup (144 g) sugar
1 teaspoon (5 ml) vanilla extract
1 cup (236 ml) sour cream
½ cup (118 ml) heavy cream
Pinch of salt

Place all ingredients in a food processor and blend until smooth. Freeze in ice cream maker according to manufacturer's instructions. Transfer to a bowl, cover, and place in freezer until firm.

JALAPEÑO ICE CREAM

An easy, and surprising, end to a spicy meal. Serve with authentic Mexican polvorones.

4 jalapeños, split and seeds removed
2 tablespoons (30 ml) lime juice
1 quart (1.25 kg) vanilla ice cream, softened

Blanch jalapeños in boiling water for 3 minutes, then transfer to a bowl of ice water. When cool, place jalapeños in blender with lime juice and process until finely diced. Place softened ice cream in a bowl and mix in the jalapeño mixture so it is thoroughly incorporated. Place in resealable container and return to freezer. Let sit overnight before eating.

Quickly work the jalapeño mixture into the ice cream; then put the ice cream back in its container and refreeze.

ZINGY GUINNESS FLOAT

1 cup (236 ml) Guinness
Jalapeño Ice Cream, see recipes above

Pour Guinness into a pint glass and let settle until head is nearly gone. Add one scoop of ice cream at a time until the glass is full. Serve with a long-handled spoon.

BEER PAIRINGS

Beer and chili go together like . . . well, beer and chili. In fact, many chili recipes contain beer, so it is an easy matter to create a flavor bridge by serving the beer you used in your recipe. But for other general recipes, here are a few options:

Texas chili: Stout highlights the caramelized depth of the smoky chiles and beef.

Red home-style chili: Amber ale has just enough sweetness to match the smoke and gentle spiciness of tomatoes, ground beef, and beans.

Chili with cinnamon and chocolate undertone: Dark and spicy porter is a match made in heaven.

Green chili with pork, white bean or tomatillos: American lager's crisp, dry finish complements the sweet pork.

White bean and chicken chili, seafood chili: Wheat ale, with just a hint of citrus, works well here.

WINE PAIRINGS

Pairing chili with wine may not seem like a natural choice, but if you are a dedicated wine drinker, there are a range of options. The bolder red chili recipes generally match well with the rustic, fruity reds, while the lighter green and white chili recipes seek out the bright green and lemony flavor in the crisp whites. Here is a sampling of possibilities:

Texas chili: a full flavored Zinfandel to match the rustic, spicy structure of the chili

Red Home-style chili: Beaujolais. Fruity complement that helps to knock down the spiciness

Chili with cinnamon and chocolate undertones: Petit Sirah's own fruitiness enhances the chili's dark flavors.

Green chili with pork, white bean or tomatillos: bright green flavor of Sauvignon Blanc plays up green chiles

White bean and chicken chili or seafood chili: Light lemony flavor of Pinot Grigio a good match

Glossary

Aji Amarillo Chile: Mild to medium heat with a fruity, tropical flavor.

Anaheim: Large chiles that can be used green or red, with a sweet, pungent, earthy flavor. Also sometimes called New Mexico's; this mild chile that forms the basis of many traditional chili recipes.

Ancho: A dried poblana. The Ancho is the sweetest of the dried chiles, making it perfect for red chili. Mildly spicy with a dark coffee-like bite.

Bell pepper: the standard sweet pepper, 0 on the Scoville scale. Available in red, yellow or green.

Bhut Jolokia: also known as the ghost chile.

Cascabel: Small, deep red chile known for its loose seeds that rattle when shaken. Nutty and medium hot with a slightly smoky flavor.

California chile: a variation of the New Mexico chile.

Capsaicin: the chemical compound that accounts for the heat in chiles.

Capsicum: the genus to which all chiles belong

Cayenne pepper: Thin hot chile pepper, can be used green or ripe. Commonly available in dried powder.

Chilaca: Long, thin medium hot chile.

Chile pepper: a category of peppers in the capsicum family.

Chile negro: also known as pasilla.

Chili: a stew commonly made with meat and chili spices.

Chile blend: A combination of common spices used for making chili. Also known as chili powder.

Chile paste: a paste made from reconstituteed dried chiles.

Chile powder: also known as ground chile.

Chili powder: a blend of ground chile and other spices, commonly cumin, garlic powder, oregano and salt.

Chimayo: classic New Mexico chile

Chipotle: A red ripe jalapeno smoked over mesquite. The popular chipotle provides a smoky earthiness with underlying heat.

Chorizo: spicy pork sausage used for Mexican and Spanish recipes

Cilantro: The fresh herb that is dried to make cumin. Fresh cilantro has a fresh aroma and a slightly bitter taste.

Cubanelle: Technically a sweet pepper, but can carry a little spice. Generally picked when yellowish-green but can ripen to red.

Cumin: aromatic spice common to chili recipes, and generally found in chili powders.

De arbol: Very hot red dried chili that can substitute easily for cayenne.

Guajillo: Smokier and spicier than the Ancho, but with a fruity tanginess that surprises. A dried form of the mirasol chile.

Ghost chile: Not so common, but worth noting. The Ghost Chile is arguably the hottest chile in the world.

Ground Chile: a ground form of one chile variety

Habanero: Fiery hot and not for the faint of heart. A little goes a long way.

Hatch chile: Mild to medium hot chiles grown in the Hatch Valley of New Mexico, generally picked green.

Jalapeño: A hot green chile that is larger than a serrano. Red jalapeños are somewhat milder.

Mexican oregano: not to be confused with its Mediterranean cousin, the Mexican version is actually a type of marjoram. More fragrant with an earthier flavor well-suited to chili recipes.

Mirasol chile: Dried to make guajillos, the most common chile for mole sauces.

Mole: a dark sauce made with chiles and unsweetened chocolate.

Mulato: a dried Poblano, but with a smokier flavor than the ancho.

New Mexico: Large chiles that can be used green or red, with a sweet, pungent, earthy flavor. Also sometimes called Anaheim's; this mild chile that forms the basis of many traditional chili recipes.

Pasila: A dried chilaca pepper that is spicy with a bitter undertone.

Pecos Red: a classic mild ground chile that makes a great chili base.

Poblano: A larger fresh green chile often used for roasting and stuffing.

Ristra: a string of dried chiles

Scotch Bonnet: One of the hottest chiles–a variation of the habanero.

Scoville Scale: a scale created to decribe the relative heat of chiles.

Serrano: A small green chile that is quite hot.

Sonnaro: large variation of an Anaheim chile.

Tabasco pepper: Hot yellow or red pepper, commonly used to make tabasco sauce.

Tomatillo: a small tomato-like vegetable in the gooseberry family. Used in fresh green salsas.

Chili Organizations and Publications

CHILI APPRECIATION SOCIETY INTERNATIONAL

The Chili Appreciation Society International (CASI) raises money for charity through the promotion of American red chili. CASI sanctions over 500 chili cook offs internationally each year as qualifying events for the Terlingua International Chili Championship. This grand spectacle is held the first Saturday of November each year at the society's grounds in Terlingua, Texas.

www.chili.org

INTERNATIONAL CHILI SOCIETY

The International Chili Society (ICS) is a non-profit organization that sanctions chili cookoffs with judging and cooking rules and regulations. These events are world-wide and benefit charities or non-profit organizations. All winners of ICS sanctioned cookoffs qualify to compete for cash prizes and awards at the World's Championship Chili Cookoff held each year in October. The ICS is the largest food contest, festival organization in the world.

www.chilicookoff.com

FIERY FOODS AND BARBECUE SUPERSITE

A website devoted to chiles and all sorts of fiery foods.
P.O. Box 4980
Albequerque, NM 87196
505-873-8680
www.fiery-foods.com

CHILE PEPPER MAGAZINE

For all things chile.
www.chilepepper.com

Resources

There are lots of places to buy dried chiles, from your local gourmet shop to Mexican markets. These are a few of my on-line favorites.

Hatch Chili Express
Authentic fresh, frozen and roasted New Mexico green chiles, green chile powders and ristras.
P.O. Box 350
Hatch, NM 87937
800-292-4454
www.hatch-chile.com

Mild Bill's Spice Company
High quality variety of chili powders and blends.
PO Box 1303
Ennis, TX 75120
972-875-2975
www.mildbills.com

New Mexican Connection
for fresh and frozen green chiles
800-933-2736
www.newmexicanconnection.com

Pendery's
All-round resource for any chile you can name, and many you can't!
1221 Manufacturing Street
Dallas, TX
800-533-1870
www.penderys.com

Penzey's
Ground chiles and chili powder, along with a wide variety of other spices.
12001 W Capital Drive
Wauwatosa, WI
800-741-7787
www.penzeys.com

Pepper Joe's
Chile pepper seed resource.
725 Carolina Farms Blvd
Myrtle Beach, SC 29579
843-742-5116
www.pepperjoe.com

Purcell Mountain Farms
The best in beans, corns, and specialty rices, along with chile powders.
Moyie Springs, Idaho
208-267-0627
www.purcellmountainfarms.com

The Chile Woman
The best resource for chile seedlings and pepper plants.
1704 S. Weimer Road
Bloomington, IN 47403
812-339-8321
www.thechilewoman.com

The Chile Shop
Wreaths, ristras, and a great assortment of green chile products.
109 E Water St
Santa Fe NM 87501
505-983-6080
www.thechileshop.com

Index

INDEX